# Because of Patty

## Paula Montgomery

REVIEW AND HERALD® PUBLISHING ASSOCIATION
HAGERSTOWN, MD 21740

The author assumes full responsibility for the accuracy of all facts and quotations as cited in this book.

This book was
Edited by Barbara Jackson-Hall
Designed by Bill Kirstein
Cover Design by Lee Cherry
Type set: 11/12 Sabon


PRINTED IN U.S.A.

96 95 94 93 92 91                    10 9 8 7 6 5 4 3 2 1



Library of Congress Cataloging in Publication Data
Montgomery, Paula.
   Because of Patty / Paula Montgomery.
       p.  cm.
   1. Bailey, Patty—Health. 2. Cerebral palsied children—
United States—Biography. 3. Cerebral palsied children—
Family relationships. 4. Bailey family. I. Title.
RJ496.C4M66  1991
362.1'9892836'0092—dc20
[B]                                        91-30546
                                           CIP

ISBN 0-8280-0646-6

DEDICATED TO

my brothers,
Sam and Roger,
and to my sister, Carme,
that you might understand how
one fragile child
helped shape our lives.

# Contents

# CHAPTER

# 1

The young intern wasted no words. "There's nothing we can do for your daughter, Mrs. Bailey. All tests indicate that Patty's condition will slowly worsen until she's a human vegetable. You should consider placing her in an institution soon, so you'll be free to care for the rest of your family."

The icy phrases struck Mella Bailey with force—numbing her. "That can't be possible," she protested, her throat dry. "Patty's always been so smart . . . she walked early—everything! You must be wrong."

The man's voice droned on. "The neurologist left a prescription at the nurse's desk. Phenobarbital. It'll help calm her when she gets bad. One teaspoon in a glass of water . . ."

Avoiding the intern's gaze, Mella grunted a reply of sorts. Her legs felt rubbery as she dragged herself to the desk for the prescription, then on to the room where Patty waited.

Mom Bert, her mother-in-law, followed silently, feeling irritated at the intern and his blunt way of breaking the news. But she struggled to accept it, fighting off the urge to cry.

All the while Mella's thoughts whirled. She knew that somewhere someone would have a cure. She knew her Patty would walk normally again and she would chatter as before. *She* wasn't about to give up!

Suddenly, Mella found herself confronted by a tiny, frail form, black-and-blue needle marks covering her arms and legs. Was this her Patty, her 2-year-old? The girl's large eyes seemed pushed deep into her skull; she was listless, unresponsive to her mother's voice. Her elfin mouth, always eager with smiles, looked drawn and blanched. Only her hair remained unchanged, its bright curls spilling over Patty's forehead like the halo it had always been.

Mella felt the sting of tears in her eyes, then turned to see them flowing freely down Mom Bert's cheeks.

"Come!" Mom Bert said, her words soothing in that cold, aseptic place. "We'll take our Patty home where she belongs."

The car soon headed southeast with Mella clutching the steering wheel. At her side Mom Bert held Patty, both women wrapped in memories that reached back two short years.

Mella felt awkward, cradling her newborn in her arms. "Patricia Agnes Bailey." She repeated the name, trying to get used to the sound and to the idea that this baby was truly hers.

Mella smiled. Being a parent offered an enchantment all its own; delightful, fresh sensations seemed to flirt with her. "I've held other children, but have never felt like this," she said quietly to herself.

Leaning back against the hospital bed, her dark eyes shining, Mella breathed, "Oh, Sam! I wish you were here. You'd be so proud."

In her imagination the tall man stood by her side. She pictured his hazel eyes, their way of talking to her. "Look what you've done for us," they'd say, "brought this beautiful daughter into the world." She caught herself reaching out for his strong hand. How she longed to feel his closeness now. She needed to share this moment with him.

But he wasn't there, and wouldn't be for several months. It was April, 1944, when the war separated many families. So the new mother consoled herself, knowing that hundreds of American brides were also without their husbands, bearing childbirth's same bittersweet pangs.

"I'll write your daddy today and take your picture to send along with the letter," she promised the infant. "That'll give our sailor something to brag about to his buddies."

Little Patty, seemingly unaffected by her importance, nestled down into her mother's robe and fell asleep.

"Oooo! Mella!" came a voice, slightly Italian, from the doorway. "She has fat on her bones. Mama will like that. 'A good sign,' she'll say."

Mella, turning to find her pretty sister tiptoeing in scolded, "Clida, shame on you! You're not supposed to come in here now with the babies. The nurse will—"

"I wasn't supposed to visit you yesterday either. But a few dollars to the cleaning lady changed that."

"Clida! I've never known you to do such a thing."

Peering anxiously at the woman and child in the other bed, Clida took her sister's hand. "Listen, your labor lasted so long—days! None of us knew if you were still alive. They told us nothing." She lowered her voice. "Do you remember, little sister? Do you remember my being here with you?"

To Mella's nod, she continued, "You were so alone. I had Johnny, but you had no one. So much pain and no one you loved nearby. You were a pitiful sight."

"Yes, it was a long labor, but she's here now. Look! Isn't she beautiful?"

Clida bent to admire her niece and to fuss a little, taking care not to waken her. Then squeezing Mella's hand and giving her a look that only sisters understand, she quickly left.

The days that followed passed quietly, except for the few times Clida and Mella's other sister, Tina, slipped away from their own families to admire the new baby in the hospital. Mella always felt amused at their raving, typical of her Italian family. Never was anything ordinary, but so beautiful, as Patty was compared with all her relatives.

"The smile is certainly her *zio's*" a family member would say, "but the nose is like *Zia* . . ." They would carry on until the new mother laughed aloud. She realized they meant well, and loved them for it, but secretly she saw only her dear husband in the small face.

A surprise walked in during the last hours of Mella's hospital stay.

"Mom Bert! What are you doing here in Detroit, all the way from Virginia?"

The older woman looked pleased and kissed her daughter-in-law. "You didn't think I could stay away from my latest grandchild, now did you?"

Mella, beaming up at her, for once was speechless. She had an unusual fondness for her husband's only parent.

Because of Mom Bert's youthful looks, no one would guess the woman's harsh past, that she had been widowed at an early age. Left on the Texas plains, she alone raised Mella's Sam and four other children.

Her soft eyes said nothing of the Depression, of the long days of work for little pay, of the regret she felt watching her sons forced into manhood before their time. Mella genuinely loved her and what she called Mom Bert's "saintly stubbornness." Surely, that stubbornness had helped her weather those hard years.

Now, perhaps, some of that same strength would support Mella during her own trial. *Without question*, Mella thought, *there will be plenty of help—three grandparents to spoil Patty!*

The first evening Mella and Patty were home, the house on Illinois Street seemed to smile through its oversized windows because of the new baby inside. Mella was perched on the living room couch, firmly placed there by her mother, or Nonna [*grandmother* in Italian] as everyone called her.

"I don'ta want you walkin' around," Nonna ordered in her Italian accent. "It'sa too soon after da baby." Then out the old woman breezed, ever keeping watch on her daughter from the other room.

Mella chuckled to herself about the differences between the two women attending her. There sat the slim Mom Bert, her silver hair wrapped neatly around her head in thick braids. Mainly of British descent, she was gracious and soft-spoken. What a contrast to Nonna. Short and plump, Nonna was a woman of perpetual motion. Her hair, more brown than gray, hung in one long braid, except when she was pinning it back up.

A thick accent never slowed her English any, and when speaking Italian, Nonna could outchatter a magpie, all the while expressing her surprise, misery, joy, and anxiety, of which she was so oddly composed. Nonna's vivacious spirit kept her house humming, and some obsession seemed to compel her flour-caked hands to the breadboard where she turned out delicacies that were neighborhood famous.

Nonna may have thought she ruled the roost, but her husband, called Noonoon, usually managed his wants in a subtle way. The old man's steadfast, easygoing presence in the background seemed to neutralize Nonna's frenzy, keeping their household on an even keel. His dark, creased face, with its handlebar mustache, revealed hard years, yet there was contradictory tenderness about it. Winter or summer, Noonoon sported a wool vest and was never without his well-worn cap outdoors.

Now Patty was there, touching each of their lives differently, yet binding the grandparents.

At first Mella had worried about how Mom Bert might react to her unorthodox family. When even part of Mella's family came around, there was a continuous high-pitched din of female voices that Mella thought would certainly offend the more refined woman. But Mom Bert remained undisturbed, ever appreciative of their hospitality. She seemed to realize the kitchen was Nonna's private domain and wisely kept from underfoot.

The days passed too quickly. Soon the time came for Mom Bert to return home. Mella, watching the gentlewoman step through the doorway, felt a part of her husband was going. Suddenly, the need for him rallied. Memories rushed upon her, leaving her emotions raw, exposed.

Unable to cope with Nonna's "I-told-you-so" looks, Mella fled to her room. She knew what her mother was thinking, that Mella was only reaping the consequences of her deed, that of forming an unholy union with Sam. Mella was considered the family rebel, marrying an outsider, a non-Italian, a Protestant, and worst of all—a sailor! The neighbor women had gossiped about it. "What a shame for Agnes' youngest to marry one of those lusty breeds!" No amount of Sam's good nature or faithfulness would reverse their judgment.

Through her tears Mella barely recognized the figure standing beside Patty's bassinet. "Oh, Pa!" She rushed to the man, her sobs storming his shoulder.

Noonoon nodded, patting his daughter's black hair. "I know, I know, Meline. Is good to cry after da baby. All womans do. I been waiting. You keep it in bottle inside you. Now it come. Is good."

"I miss Sam so much," Mella cried. For a time she became a little girl again, revealing her deepest hurts to her father who always understood. With his broken English he helped put her shattered self together once more. "Stony steps," he called troublesome times, "to makea you a better person."

After a while Noonoon left his daughter with some gentle advice. "You cry now. Get it all out. Den be strong for your *bambina*. She is part of your *marito*, here for you 'till he comesa home."

Mella gazed down at her sleeping baby, the little one innocent and unaware of the cruel war that had driven a wedge into the heart of her family. Contented in her tiny world, Patty slept on.

"When will your father get home to see you?" Mella whispered to her child. There was no way of knowing. Sam never mentioned his whereabouts in his letters. It was against regulations, and despite how careful Sam was, the censor still marked out words, making the pages look unloving.

Suddenly, Nonna's soprano voice broke into Mella's thoughts. From the kitchen came fiery words, noisily scolding Noonoon.

A faint smile brushed across Mella's lips. She realized that the saucy outburst was her mother's way of saying, "I care also!" only she was too proud to admit it. And with the smile came a host of positive thoughts to bolster her morale. Again

12

Mella was herself. Again she would have to wait patiently for her husband's return.

When Patty turned 6 weeks old, Mella wrote in the baby book: *My first outing: Patricia and Mother went to visit the doctor . . . He said I was healthy.*

But within a few weeks after the checkup, Patty experienced projectile vomiting at times.

Nonna, with her stockpile of omens, shook a plump finger at her daughter. "Dat's a bad sign," she warned. "You will see someday!"

# CHAPTER

# 2

For weeks Sam Bailey's shipmates aboard the U.S.S. *Phoenix* had teased him at mail call. "Are we uncles or aunts?"

When news finally did reach him somewhere in the Southwest Pacific, Sam hastily opened the letter on his way back to quarters and voiced his triumph in an unquestionably Texan, "Yippee!" Then popping into sick bay, he hollered, "You're aunts!"

A commotion followed, his friends mobbing him as they commented on the snapshots. "What a good-looker, Sam!" and "It's about time!" In sharing the new father's joy, each sailor felt the moment in his own way. A few of them had been out to sea when their children had been born. They knew the same opposing thrill and sadness, the awful frustration of a father half a world away from his firstborn.

When the merriment subsided, Sam was free to study the letter in more detail. Patricia Agnes had been born on April 11, a few weeks before. Mella went on about all the details that mean so much to parents. She included the news of Mom Bert's visit and about everyone's health, but Sam skimmed over those parts, reviewing only the description of Patty, while glancing at her pictures. *She's a fat little rascal, Sam. Except for her dark eyes, she favors you. What little hair she has looks blonde. Can't believe it, dear! I don't think there's ever been a blonde Serri.*

Sam practically memorized every word before putting the

letter aside and fastening the photos of his "pin-up girl" to his locker.

Having some time before sick call, he lay back down on his bunk and stared at the ceiling. *I'm a father*, he mused, feeling almost smug.

His childhood flashed before him—his baby sister, Jamie, waddling her first step, displaying a toothless grin, her small, awkward self, the family's pride. Sam gazed back at Patty's picture and tried to imagine his own daughter in Jamie's place, but to no avail. The surroundings robbed him of his daydreams. He could hear sounds in the corridor—footsteps, occasional laughter, the rattle of chains as men moved up and down ladders.

Only a few sailors remained with him in the compartment now. One man in skivvies was sprawled atop his bunk across from Sam. Others were quietly readying supplies for sick call. The cold, steel walls, their painted rivets jutting out uniformly, seemed like a prison with the cloud of cigarette smoke hovering at the ceiling.

Wanting to be alone with his thoughts, to breathe fresh air, and see beyond those smothering quarters, Sam climbed topside.

Reclining against a gun turret, the young sailor gazed seaward. On the battleship's downward roll he watched the waves, their tongues lapping up at heavy clouds that selfishly covered the sky. Again he knew confinement. Trying to peer beyond nature's walls, he felt the miles stretched endlessly between himself and his loved ones.

It pained Sam to think that he could not hold his daughter while she was tiny. "She could be half grown before I get to see her," he grumbled. He longed for the orders that would send him stateside, where he could do away with his imaginings and really hold his little girl.

While his mind still lingered on Patty and on his wife's loving words, the ship's seesawing lulled him to sleep.

In Detroit, sleep eluded Mella at times, especially during a long spell between letters. She knew it wasn't Sam's fault.

He had always been faithful in writing—more than she, in fact. But during those war-torn days, the postal service was interrupted occasionally, and then there would come a flood of letters from her Sam.

That particular night Mella had finished Patty's late feeding, and after an hour of restless tossing, crept into her parents' living room to sit alone awhile in the stillness.

A streetlamp cast its faint glow on the old, flowered wallpaper that climbed high around the room. Scars from many years of wear on the carpet and furnishings seemed hidden in the dimness. Everything that she had known from childhood looked unchanged. Even the odor of coal was there. The familiarity of it all was comforting.

She could almost see her father sitting in the corner, a stogie flopping under his mustache as he played the concertina or "squeeze box" as the children had called it. The 10 boarders living upstairs would join them. Those times had been so merry, people laughing and singing, everyone doing his or her best to forget the awful Depression lurking outside. In that house they had been safe with their food, their friends, their music.

"Oh, the music!" Mella sighed as she remembered all the concerts born in that very room—the accordion, clarinets, guitars, their melodies rippling into early morning hours.

Oddly enough, Prohibition hadn't seemed to affect their old-country ways much. Nonna had continued making wine. There was an incident, however, in Pennsylvania, before the family had moved to Detroit. When Mella thought about it, her chuckle pierced the house's silence.

Nonna had busily collected elderberry juice for wine one day. After some hours, its inviting aroma floated out into the neighborhood.

"The Revenue Men are coming!" one of her girls warned as she raced into the kitchen where Nonna was laboring beside a large barrel, nearly brimful by that time.

Nonna gasped *"Carabiniere!"*

Within minutes the men stomped up the front porch steps and into the house, without knocking. Determined to catch the woman in her unlawful act, they followed the scent into the kitchen.

As if to challenge them, there stood the barrel in the midst of the room, an untidy pile of clothes strewed alongside, and Nonna's head peeking out of the dark brew.

She shrieked, "How dare you stop my bath! Cannot you see I bathing in wine for my health?"

The shock and embarrassment of the intruders was obvious. Stammering apologies, the Revenuers retreated, never to return.

In that moment Mella realized her mother's years of hardship, the daily cooking for all the boarders upstairs, keeping them from starving during the Depression, along with caring for her own large family. Certainly, it had been a genuine labor of love, enduring the tedious work day after day. Mella had been too young to appreciate it then. But now she was aware and suddenly loving her mother anew.

Gazing for a last time at the dimly lit room, Mella sensed the simple emotion, the unguarded love, the rousing songs that still lingered within those walls—memories that created her very being. Now her child lay in this house so full of her own life.

Mella tiptoed back to the empty bed where, just an hour before, fear had rankled her. "Please, God," she prayed, "bring Sam back safely. Let him have the chance to hold Patty—please!"

With that, she drifted off into a deep and restful sleep.

When Sam's ship finally anchored in Seattle, Mella was ecstatic. She hurried up the stairs to the bedroom where 4-month-old Patty lay on the double bed among stacks of freshly laundered diapers.

"Your daddy's coming, little girl. He's really coming home!" Dizzy in her delight, she bounced the child on the mattress, then squeezed her wriggling body. The diapers tumbled onto Patty's moist skin, giving the baby short relief from Detroit's summer swelter. Patty cooed an approval, her blonde curls joggling merrily atop her head. Then she clutched at a lock of her mother's hair.

"Ouch! That's no way to treat me," Mella protested, teasing and tickling the baby girl, making her giggle.

It was August. Residential streets were mostly deserted. People avoided the feverish sidewalks, keeping their shades drawn in the daytime. But the heat would gradually creep into their homes, and by evening, dwellers lined their front porches. Even little Patty, wrapped in an apron, was allowed the brief pleasure of sitting outside on Noonoon's lap. She could revel in sights of lively children ducking in alleyways and moths fluttering atop streetlamps. Then, long after the sleepy cherub was bedded down, grownups outside would chatter until late, spilling laughter at times, concealing their dread of the next day's muggy heat.

Mella dashed out the door, leaving Patty to complain loudly on the couch. Tina rushed to comfort her niece, happy for the opportunity. Nothing, not even her own child's tears, could dampen Mella's spirits. Her Sam was coming home! The car's motor was singing it. Even a quick-stepping pedestrian was dancing it. Mella sensed the city rejoicing with her as she guided the car through knotted traffic that at any other time would have been unnerving. But not today. Today her Sam was returning, who by rights had been her husband for 16 months, but in reality for three, the first three and only months they had together before orders sent him overseas.

Mella began to prod herself with questions. *Does he still look like himself? Is he the same lighthearted Sam, or has the war left him withdrawn and disillusioned?* She had heard stories of shell-shocked husbands returning from the war zone, of their agony and that of their families. Had her husband also been affected?

"Sam mustn't be different," Mella breathed.

Although worlds apart in background and faith, Sam and Mella's personalities complemented each other. Where she was weak, he possessed strength. To counter her moodiness, he had a certain stability. Without Sam's stamina Mella knew she would crumble.

Soon she was making her way through the terminal,

meeting happy faces of servicemen arm-in-arm with loved ones.

*His plane's in. I must be late.* Breathlessly, Mella neared the gate, more and more uniforms collecting before her. Then through them she spotted a familiar sight, as if she had known it all of her life—his back, the Navy garb fitting just the same, his dark auburn hair tucked under a sailor's cap. Gathering every lonesome hour away from her husband into words, Mella whispered, "Sam!"

In that instant Sam turned as if responding to her call. He darted clumsily among the crowd. Then, oblivious to onlookers, he enfolded his wife and kissed her lips already salty with tears.

"Oh, Sam!" Mella sobbed. "I wasn't going to cry. My makeup. I'll look dreadful."

"You're beautiful, darling, just beautiful!"

In no time they were battling Detroit's traffic, heading toward the Serri house on Illinois Street. Hastily parking the car, Sam left his wife behind, and taking the front steps three at a time, bounded into the living room.

"There's my gal!" He grinned at the small, grumpy face on the couch.

When Mella came in, she stood with her mouth open. Sam had already pulled off Patty's bonnet, her dress, and was soon to disrobe Patty to her diapers. *How could he do that—after all my trouble to dress her so perfectly?* Mella smiled to herself.

"There. How's my gal now?" Sam asked with a certain paternal air.

Gurgling a definite "Thank you," the little one fell in love with her father at once.

The Serri clan had been waiting for Sam to return to Detroit so that Patty could be baptized, a joyous occasion for them—but not for the young father.

The moment for promisekeeping had arrived, and he dreaded the consequences. Catholic pomp clashed with his conservative Protestant upbringing. Besides, St. Elizabeth's sanctuary bore little resemblance to the simple, country worship place of his childhood.

Feeling like a misfit, Sam tried to conceal his apprehension as he sat alongside mirthful relatives. His uneasiness grew with the echoing footsteps of the priest nearing the gathering. Sam then heard strange, Latin syllables, the alien ceremony seeming anything but holy to the sailor.

Noonoon glanced at the distressed father every now and then, the old man's eyes twinkling with perception. Noonoon, more than anyone, realized what a mismatch his Meline and Sam were. He had approved of the union, though, realizing that Sam had a love tough enough for a lifetime. Noonoon seemed amused at his son-in-law's suffering, thinking it a good lesson for the undoubtedly rocky path ahead.

Finally it was time for Clida to hand the baby to the priest for the actual christening.

A noise came from the child. "Daddy!" She was barely 5 months old, surely too young to talk, but the sound was *Daddy* to Sam, a cry for help adding to his own anguish. At that moment every muscle in his body was set to spring for Patty, to carry her away, but then his eyes met Mella's. She smiled reassuringly, then sympathetically, as if to say, "Do it for me, darling. You know how much it means, and I know how hard this is for you." Did she know? Could she even partly understand his agony?

One last look at his daughter squalling over the baptismal font, and Sam settled back to witness the rest of the ceremony.

Days would pass before he could put his feelings into words, words that Mella would try to understand.

Saturday morning brought with it the weekly chore of making tortulinis, the Serri's favorite memento of their homeland. Mella busily measured flour for the egg dough while Nonna ground chicken for the filling. All the while the older woman outtalked her daughter saying, as she did every

Saturday morning, that this was the best chicken she had ever raised.

Their kitchen chatter had been mostly Italian since Sam was away. Mella had carefully guarded her spouse's feelings, wanting him to be included in all conversation, and sometimes, she had to reprimand her wily mother for talking "behind Sam's back" in the native tongue. Mella was just reaching into the canister for more flour when familiar steps on the living room floor stopped her.

"Sam, is that you?" she called.

When a sober face greeted Mella, her countenance fell. "Don't tell me—you've gotten your orders," her eyes filling rapidly with tears. "They're going to send you away from me already?"

Sam blushed, never expecting his wife to cry. "Not yet. My orders are for Norfolk, Virginia—and you and Patty will come along."

"Oh Sam!" Mella exclaimed as she embraced her husband, spreading tortulini dough across the back of his neck.

Sam grunted a protest. "Watch the hands!"

"Serves you right, you big brute! Shame on you for leading me on like that!" Mella deliberately dabbed some of the sticky stuff on his nose. Sam quickly fled up the stairway to wash and to avoid any more of his wife's antics.

The two women continued their task, but Nonna's mood had changed abruptly. Her sullen face showed disapproval at Mella's leaving. Not one of her children had ever moved from Detroit. The family had always been there, frequently returning to the big house on Illinois Street, reminding Nonna that she was needed and loved. This new turn caught her off guard. How she longed to throw her arms around Mella, using loving words to convince her to stay. But that was against her nature, so Nonna kept silent, thinking up excuses to persuade Meline later on.

The next day some of the family gathered after Mass at the Serri place to enjoy Sunday dinner. The men slouched comfortably in the living room where Noonoon was nursing his all-day stogie. The cigar's pungent odor wafted through the rooms, clashing with the sweet aroma of broth and cheese from the kitchen. It didn't bother the womenfolk, whose clatter of tongues outdid any distractions.

"How will you go down to Virginia, Mella?" Tina asked while setting the dining room table.

"Sam's to get train tickets. He's hoping for a sleeping compartment part of the way."

"Nice!"

Nonna scowled. The plans sounded threatening. "Meline, da *bambina* is so little. You can stay here awhile, den go to Sam later," she coaxed.

"Sorry, Ma. My place is with my husband. Anyway, we hope to visit his mother in Arlington for a week before dropping down to Norfolk."

"But da polio sickness is in da cities now. You should keep Patty away from peoples."

Polio! The older woman had struck a nerve, reminding them of the disease that was leaving a trail of death and paralysis across the nation. Each time Mella had taken Patty out in the baby carriage, she shied away from groups of children playing along sidewalks, thinking one of them might be carrying the dreaded sickness.

"Don't worry, Ma," Mella said, dismissing her fears. "God will watch over our Patty. We'll all pray, huh?"

Nonna replied with a shrug, "I don'ta tink God wants us to be stupid."

Despite Nonna's protests the next few days, the Bailey trio still managed to get to the train depot. Mella's brother, Carlo, took Nonna and Noonoon along for the farewell.

Upon boarding, Mella looked at her parents. There stood the dear couple on the platform, looking like an out-of-place replica from the old country decorating a large knickknack shelf. Noonoon wore the woolen vest and cap as always, while Nonna sported her several sweaters, both of them apparently oblivious to August's heat wave.

Suddenly, it dawned upon Mella that except for a vacation with her father in San Diego, she was leaving home for the first time, the only one in her family to dare such a thing.

When she looked at Carlo, he seemed to cheer her on with, "Good for you, Mella," yet a trace of envy colored the sadness in his eyes.

Mella watched tenderly, choking back tears while Nonna squeezed Patty. *"Vaya con Dios,* little one." The grandmother was struggling to keep her tough exterior.

And Noonoon, too, looked misty-eyed. Mella hugged the old man. "Remember, Pa, you and Ma come and visit us this winter. It's not so rough in Virginia. We'll be expecting you."

One last goodbye, then Sam, Mella, and Patty boarded the sleeper car, leaving the elderly twosome huddled together, waving continuously.

A porter helped Sam with the luggage and directed them to their compartment. Mella laid Patty down on the bottom berth and looked glumly out the window. The outskirts of the city rushed past her, a city she was leaving behind.

As soon as the porter left, Sam took Mella in his arms, trying to counter her blues. "How's this for class, ma'am?" He grinned roguishly. "Did you notice that we have our own private head?" He swung open the narrow door, revealing the toilet.

"La di da!" Mella deliberately acted cheerful while fingering the sink fixtures and primping in front of the mirror.

Sam admired her reflection and wondered, *Would a woman with such strong family ties be able to adjust to this new lifestyle?* He knew they would be on the move constantly, always resetting up housekeeping, making new friends, only to separate again. But he also realized that his wife's greatest asset was her love of people. He expected that her friendships would be precious to her wherever the Navy sent them.

Anyway, time would supply his answers.

# CHAPTER

# 3

Months passed slowly under Virginia's autumn sunshine. Except for Mrs. Pierson, the landlady, who kept the tenants on edge with her regimental ways, military life agreed with Mella. She was pregnant again and content just knowing that Sam would be close this time. She wasn't going to allow the hard-crusted landlady, with a "here-am-I" air to spoil this experience for her.

And Patty's personality was developing so that Mella increasingly enjoyed her.

Mella was able to cope with any homesickness that tried to undo her—until Christmas Day. She made an attempt to look cheerful, trying to forget the awful gnawing at her heart, the nostalgia that drove her thoughts to the big house in Detroit. She pictured her family all there together and longed for them, especially their emotion-charged evenings.

At least with them, when depression came, Mella could escape to the old piano, its soothing notes accompanying her tearful songs. But in this new home there was no piano, only Mrs. Pierson to scrutinize her every move.

Like the perfect remedy, a letter arrived a few days after Christmas saying that the elder Serris were packing for Virginia. Mella was delighted, knowing her folks would bring a bit of her past and the "homeplace" with them.

"Well, that settles it, Mella," Sam announced. "We'll have to move. There's no way your mother and Mrs. Pierson could ever cook under the same roof." He grinned. "Can't you just see Mrs. Pierson the first time she discovered a headless chicken draining from the faucet?" Then Sam laughed so loudly that Mella feared an eavesdropping Mrs. Pierson might oust them ahead of time.

Sam found a rather worn duplex that required much cleaning, but it was roomy enough so they moved in.

The highlight of every evening was Sam's return from work. Patty recognized the sounds in the living room that brought her tiny-stepping, clinging to furniture all the way to the familiar black shoes. She would tug on her father's pant leg, gaze up at him and wait for the great moment when the uniformed sailor would sweep her into his arms. The little deceiver knew that *she* was the one in control, the one who had scooped him into *her* arms, holding him there with her charm.

After supper Sam would try to read the paper. This was the time for Patty's attention-getting routine, her mischievous eyes shining as she would make her way to the paper and punch it. Clutching her father's knee, she would pester him until he tossed the paper aside. The paper could wait. Now was the time when he could grab his grinning girl and toss her in the air. Her blonde hair would fall back to cheeks puffed out with giggles. Patty was growing taller now, the baby fat disappearing.

One evening Sam's voice boomed from the doorway, "Surprise!"

Mella jumped up. "Pa! Ma!" She ran to her parents, hugging them both at once.

After supper, while dishes were being washed, Nonna rattled on, hardly stopping for breath in order to convey all the details of their train trip.

Sam was filling the coal stove when they settled down afterward. "Seems warmer in here now since you stuffed paper behind the molding, dear."

"Hush, Sam!" Mella whispered. "Do you want Ma to hear?" But Nonna wasn't interested in their secret. She was busy admiring her grandchild who rocked in the apple-crate horse, chattering. Nonna's high-pitched voice trilled, "Looka her! Senator Bailey!" The room rang with laughter. Patty did look like a miniature politician, swinging her hands and jabbering.

Mella fondly watched her loved ones, feeling snug in the warmth of the old stove and her family's nearness. She smiled at the promise of new life within her.

*Everything will be all right now*, she concluded to herself. *My folks are here.*

Summer was already upon them the morning Sam nudged his snoring mother-in-law. "Wake up, Ma! It's a girl."

A disappointed "Oooh!" came from Nonna as she rolled over, her half-open eyes scrutinizing Sam's cheery face. "Whatsa matta? You not sad you don'ta have a son?"

"Nah. We can always have another." Noticing the old woman's disapproving grunt, he quickly added, "You should see her, Ma! Just as dark as can be. In fact, she kind of looks like a monkey."

"A monkey!" With that, Nonna sat straight up in bed, grabbing her robe dramatically, all the while rebuking her son-in-law for what she thought an awful description.

Undaunted, Sam interrupted her. "We're calling her Paula for Pa."

"Ah!" The words immediately straightened the wrinkled brow. Nonna didn't smile, but Sam could tell she was pleased. Patty's middle name, Agnes, had been for her, and now this child would be called after her Leopoldo.

"And da second name?"

"Rhea, for my best buddy, Rhea Dan."

Nonna began to mutter to herself as she headed toward the kitchen. "Named for two mans. Poor *bambina*! Her papa tinks she looks lika monkey and calls her two mans' names. Poor, poor *bambina*!"

"What's that, Ma?" Sam's mouth was forming a giant yawn.

Nonna ignored his question. "Whatcha want to eat?"

At breakfast Nonna said she would stay for two more

weeks, then go back home to Noonoon. She would never admit it, but she missed the old man who had left a few weeks earlier for upper Michigan. He hoped to buy land there for his long-awaited dream cabin by a lake. Somehow Nonna felt incomplete without him, but kept her thoughts well camouflaged beneath her constant bustle.

When Mella brought Paula home, the infant was 5 days old and had hair growing right down to her already thick eyebrows.

Mella placed her carefully in the bassinet that, weeks earlier, she had decorated in yellow dotted swiss with layers of ruffles.

When Nonna first peeked at the baby she mused, "Whadda ya know? Sam wasn' lyin'. She *does* kinda look lika monkey."

One afternoon not long after the new arrival, Sam mysteriously disappeared with his sole remaining savings bond. After an hour he returned with a darling, 6-week-old cocker spaniel. Seeing his wife's disbelieving face, he explained sheepishly, "Every little girl needs a dog."

"Oh, Sam! How could you? I'm finally getting Patty toilet trained, have little Paula in diapers, and you bring home a dog to be housebroken?"

"Yeah!" He grinned in his roguish way. "Isn't she cute?"

Mella had to admit the cocker was, indeed, cute. She couldn't help smiling as she watched the puppy traipsing across the floor, exploring the new quarters. Patty was ecstatic, toddling after the dog, never quite keeping up— much to the animal's advantage!

For once Nonna said nothing. She was glad to be going home soon, away from Sam's strange gift, this little animal that she knew would do nothing but keep underfoot and make puddles throughout the house. She was also thinking about the noodle machine she had recently bought. Nonna was eager to try it out and to leave enough spaghetti behind to ease her daughter's workload.

First thing the next morning, as soon as Sam left, Nonna began to gather ingredients for the pasta, her strong, plump hands working the dough on the breadboard.

"Whatcha making, Ma?" Mella called from the other room.

"I'ma tryin' out dis new machine."

In no time at all Nonna was turning out long strings of spaghetti, hanging them to dry everywhere—over curtain rods, backs of chairs, bed posts—anything available—even the living room chandelier. There seemed no end to the spaghetti.

Mella knew better than to protest. She wisely kept Patty in her playpen and smuggled Susie, the dog, outside to protect the noodles as well as the pet.

*If anything happened to that puppy, it would break Sam's heart*, she thought, fully realizing her mother's contempt for the animal.

Finally, when the last of the spaghetti was hung on back of the couch, Nonna returned to the kitchen to prepare lunch.

Meanwhile, Sam had been bragging about his new daughter to one of his bachelor friends, a chief hospital corpsman like himself.

"Why don't you come with me for lunch and see her for yourself?" Sam invited, never suspecting that all was not ordinary on the homefront.

When the two men strolled through the door, they were stopped by a doughy contrivance at eye level. Both men looked dumbfounded as they gazed around at what looked like a small-scale spaghetti factory. Sam, who usually had excuses close at hand for Nonna's antics, stood speechless. Everywhere he turned was spaghetti—drooping, hanging, dangling, or clinging.

When Mella spotted them she began to laugh, until she doubled over in tears, bringing Nonna quickly to her side. The older woman scolded, in Italian, that Mella shouldn't be exerting herself so soon after the baby. Then, satisfied with her lecture, Nonna returned to the stove where she was preparing—of all things—spaghetti!

After an explanation they all crowded around the small table, Patty included, amid the stringy surroundings. Although Sam had joined his wife in the merriment, his poor comrade never quite recovered from the surprise. He just placidly chewed his dinner, and studied the talkative woman with the noodle machine.

Soon Nonna was on her way north, and the four Baileys were preparing for another move, this time to chief's housing at the Naval Training Center in Norfolk.

By this time Mella was used to moving and had a system worked out with boxes. She didn't regret leaving the duplex, its floor space having dwindled considerably since setting up house the winter before.

The clean, yellow exterior of chief's quarters looked homey, and the hardwood floors offered a welcomed contrast to the wrinkled linoleum left behind. With two spacious bedrooms, Mella felt they had found a real home for once. Everything seemed perfect. Nothing hinted of the awful change that would soon affect the contented family.

# 4

Old Man Winter was closing shop early that year and prickly buds were lining the trees and bushes. Soon showers, washing the greenery alongside the yellow two-stories, would make colors vivid.

Chief's quarters housed many during the few months the Baileys lived there because Sam, with his curious mixture of sympathy and family pride, was known for bringing home lonesome sailors and other strays.

Mella had adapted willingly. How well she knew homesickness. She understood their heartache, these half-grown men so newly plucked from their families, as if the uniform they donned was to banish their past and toughen them overnight. She always prepared plenty at mealtime in case Sam would pop in with a couple extra mouths to feed.

With frequent company, larger quarters to keep, and two small, but lively, children to look after, Mella never found herself idle. She kept busy in her homemaker's role, watching autumn and winter out the kitchen window as they blurred past her.

The war had ended with many victory celebrations, but the greatest celebration, Mella thought, was in her own heart. Sam might be called overseas again, but no more would the waters be under fire; no more would she lie awake nights, praying for his safety.

Although the air was warm now with spring's promise,

Mella was careful to dress the girls in coats and bonnets for a jaunt to the post dispensary. Patty would be getting her first inoculations, soon experiencing the sting that accompanied a shiny needle and a nurse's sweet voice.

In a few days it became apparent that the smallpox vaccination hadn't taken properly, so Patty was given another. This time it was successful, and Mella breathed easier, knowing that her child was protected from the scarring disease.

As Patty neared her second birthday, a change in her began, slowly, hardly noticeable at first, like a villain plotting in their midst.

In the mornings when the toddler waved her usual "bye-bye" to her daddy, at times Patty's hand would fall abruptly, bringing a puzzled, almost hurt expression to her delicate face that only moments before brimmed with smiles. Again she would try, and again her hand would fall. Mella ignored these first symptoms, brushing them aside with excuses about the early hour.

But days later when Patty was at play, the symptoms showed themselves again, and Mella couldn't ignore them any longer. Patty would look longingly at a toy, but couldn't quite coordinate to pick it up. At other times she seemed unusually clumsy as things would fall from her grasp. After about two weeks of this, Mella took Patty back to the base dispensary.

Following a brief checkup, the physician smiled. "Now, Mrs. Bailey, she's fine. Why, she's a picture of health. Just look at that peaches-and-cream complexion!"

Mella found herself agreeing with the doctor. Patty certainly did look healthy. Mella wondered if she was just a doting parent, something she had vowed never to be, letting her imagination get the best of her. So she left the doctor's office, feeling confident that Patty's strange behavior was part of some phase her daughter was passing through, soon to end.

Later, however, when Sam was gone on dispensary duty,

all the neatly discarded fears returned with one terrifying scream.

Mella raced to Patty's crib, in that instant imagining all sorts of horrors. *Had the child caught her neck in the bars somehow? Maybe somebody had hurt her. Maybe—* But all her thoughts collided with one another when Mella flicked on the light. There sat Patty beating her head against the crib, rocking back and forth, as if in a trance.

Mella lifted her, trying to quiet her, but the frenzied wail continued.

*Something* is *wrong*, Mella told herself, then shuddered when she realized that not one tear shone in her child's eyes. Patty looked stupefied, unreal.

Holding the child close, rocking the rigid body, Mella let her thoughts stray. *Was this the "someday" my mother predicted long ago? What hideous thing is trying to take over my sweet daughter?*

Finally, Patty fell asleep, and Mella, feeling drained, made her way back to her empty room. She longed for Sam, his strength, his carefree voice to calm her. As the hours passed Mella was too burdened to cry, afraid even to pray about Patty, afraid to admit aloud that some strange illness was affecting her firstborn.

The next day while Sam slept, Patty again began to scream wildly. In seconds the father was there.

"What's happened?" Mella was trying to quiet Patty, but the child kept rocking back and forth, hitting her head against the table. Again there were no tears, just the wooden stare and screaming. After two trying hours Mella and Sam were finally able to calm Patty, the ordeal showing on both their drawn faces.

"What are we going to do, Sam?"

Her husband thought for a moment. "You know my commander friend? Well, he's up on specialists in the area. I'll ask him tomorrow." Then Sam turned to his daughter, "Come here, Princess!" Patty looked weary, but managed a smile. Sliding from her mother's lap, she took a step forward, two sideways. The same puzzled expression flashed across her face, then she struggled on.

Her father didn't wait for more. He swept her into his arms. Mella wept openly. Putting his free arm around her, Sam pulled Mella close, just as a parent might comfort a troubled child. "Don't worry, honey. There's got to be a solution to this."

The next morning the commander suggested a physician at a hospital just down the road.

After an extensive examination the doctor came to the conclusion that Mella was feeding Patty too much and prescribed a diet.

But the same turbulent nights would continue to haunt them. Nights of agony for Sam and Mella. Nights filled with Patty's wild screaming and repetitive motion. Nights of taking turns between Patty and Paula, who always woke in the midst of the turmoil. Nights in which Mella cried herself to sleep and in which Sam felt frustrated with his attempts to settle her mind.

He, too, was worried. Patty had begun to chew her fingers mechanically, seeming not to feel any pain. While wrapping Patty's small hands to protect them, Sam wanted to shake himself awake, prove that this was all a nightmare, but he couldn't. He knew it was real, that little by little he was losing his spirited, talkative child, and he felt so helpless.

With a sigh, he squared his shoulders and chided himself for such thinking. He must not weaken. Mella had always leaned on him. And although these nights were robbing him of precious rest that he needed for work the next day, Sam knew he had to stay strong for his wife's sake.

Mella took Patty back to the dispensary, this time seeing a different doctor. He put the toddler down in his office and gently commanded, "Come here, Patty!"

The youngster, who knew no strangers, smiled at him, then took a step forward, two sideways, then forward again. Finally, she reached him.

The physician thought for a few moments, then said, "Looks like chorea, Mrs. Bailey. I'd like to suggest that you take her to the University of Virginia in Charlottesville. They have an excellent staff there. Maybe they can do something to help her."

For the first time in weeks Mella felt a surge of hope as she loaded her two girls into the car. "The University of Virginia!" she breathed, thinking how impressive that sounded. "They'll have the answer."

Sam accompanied Mella as they took Patty into the large university building. Patients straggled past in the corridors, and blonde, rosy-cheeked Patty looked quite healthy compared to them. Only a slight twitch at her mouth and its resulting drool gave her away.

When their appointment came, the neurologist went through the familiar examination on the child. Mella knew the routine well—the writing on a fresh chart, the silence as he contemplated, and her own heart's loud pulse as she awaited his remarks.

The doctor cleared his throat. "Mr. and Mrs. Bailey, it looks like Patty has post-encephalitis, low-grade. I'd like to keep her for a week-to-ten days for tests. Then we should have an answer for you."

Sam and Mella didn't like the thought of leaving their child, but after the necessary paperwork, they kissed Patty goodbye and walked hand-in-hand to the parking lot.

Sam, being a hospital corpsman, had enough medical knowledge to expect a dismal report, but he tried to answer Mella's questions without sounding pessimistic.

"Encephalitis," he explained, "is an inflammation of the brain."

"The doctor said 'low-grade,' Sam. That sounds encouraging then, doesn't it, honey?" Mella was searching, wanting assurance from Sam that the doctor's statement meant little harm had been done, and that Patty would be well soon.

Sam's answer, as innocent as it was, gave his wife false hope. "Seems to me, Mella."

That one shred of comfort grew into a beguiling daydream. When Mella went home and resumed her daily chores, her imagination ran wild. She could see the university doctors curing Patty, and again and again she pictured the child running straight into her arms crying, "Mama!"

As soon as the news of Patty's hospitalization reached Sam's mother in Arlington, Mom Bert headed down to Norfolk. She wanted to be at Mella's side when time came for Patty's release.

Now, as the car neared the tidewater region of Virginia, Mella considered the diagnosis. The intern's words haunted her, "*Patty's condition will slowly worsen until she's a human vegetable* . . ."

*He doesn't really know my child like I do*, Mella consoled herself, sweeping the diagnosis aside.

Mom Bert stayed a few days longer than planned to offer moral support as well as help with the physical burden. Her heart was heavy as she watched her daughter-in-law and grandchild. Those few days seemed to blot out their happy past. She wanted to stay on, to help the young family through this valley, but her job waited in Washington, D.C. Thus obligated, she left amid kisses and promises of prayers.

Mella grew to despise the phenobarbital, for the effect it had on her daughter's usually lively eyes. Those glistening, mischievous looks, the flirty glances, that were Patty's own, fled when the drug took charge, turning her eyes dull and lethargic, making Patty a stranger to her loved ones. Mella found herself holding out with the medicine until the last minute.

When that drug didn't seem to help anymore, the doctor changed to another, rotating medicines frequently.

As weeks passed Mella went about her duties methodically, taking care of the baby, the household chores, and of course, Patty. But slowly Mella withdrew from the real world that pained her.

As Patty's condition worsened, the harsh words of the intern returned again and again, "*You should consider placing her in an institution soon* . . ."

Mella prayed, begging God to stop the dreadful sickness that was ruining her child. Then one day Sam came home with a report giving his wife new hope to cling to.

"Mella, there's a Dr. Mansfield who's quite interested in Patty's case. He's a civilian, hon, and this weekend he's going to a children's hospital up north to find out about experiments they're doing with fever therapy."

Mella came alive. "Fever therapy? What is it?"

"Well, the idea is to give the patient an injection that causes her temperature to rise. They want it to go high, about 106 degrees. It's possible that it could reverse Patty's condition."

"You mean, Patty could get well?"

"Now, Mella," Sam warned, "I don't want you to get your hopes up. It's just in the experimental stage. They'll need our permission, of course. At the rate Patty's going, though, I don't see why we shouldn't try."

Mella wasn't really listening then. She was off in her dream world again, thinking that this was another chance, surely the miracle she had been praying for.

Early Monday morning Patty was checked into the hospital up north. Sam stayed by her side while Mella waited in the corridor, half reading, half praying throughout the day. Baby Paula was left in the care of a nurse friend.

Feeling a bit guilty, Sam grinned down at Patty, who seemed so small, her head nestled into the large pillow. Upon entering the doctor looked tired, his eyes showing the effects of a hurried weekend trip. A nurse following him was quite a contrast, acting pert, quick to the doctor's commands. Too soon, it seemed, the experiment was underway.

Sam cringed as the needle penetrated his daughter's flesh, the little girl whimpering. When the vein collapsed, the doctor asked for another needle. This time Patty howled, adding to both men's frustration. Finally, the injection was given, and Sam relaxed and waited. He was to take Patty's temperature every ten minutes.

She lay there in the bed fidgeting. From time to time her tear-stained face turned toward her father with a trusting smile, only making him feel more like a scoundrel.

"It's for your own good, princess," he tried to reassure her—as well as himself.

Patty's temperature climbed to 104 degrees, but stopped there. When the doctor came back in he muttered, "It's supposed to go to 106, Sam. She'll be due for another injection soon. We'll try again."

The attending nurse looked at the thermometer. "Isn't this ironic? So many times I've soaked children from head to foot, trying to get their temps down, and here I am rooting for this one to go up!"

But it didn't go any higher and after a day of futile attempts, Sam and Mella took Patty home.

Mella had greeted him at the hospital door, her anxious eyes meeting his. "Tell me, Sam! Did it work?"

"No, darling, it didn't. Her fever just wouldn't rise. The doctor couldn't understand it. I'm sorry I got your hopes up."

Mella didn't cry. She said little, once more retreating to her protective world. Sam grew more and more concerned about his wife. She had always been such an outgoing, optimistic person. When he received orders for an aircraft carrier overseas, he realized he couldn't leave her, considering her mental state.

Sam went to the Bureau of Medicine and Surgery to explain the hardship. As a result of the visit, his orders were changed to Great Lakes, Illinois, so that Mella could live closer to her family for six months.

It was good to see the young mother smile again when Sam shared the news with her. "And Mella, you'll be able to stay in Detroit with your folks while I'm at Great Lakes. I'm sure I'll be able to get weekend passes. Maybe we'll even have time to go up to Higgins Lake, to the cabin and enjoy a vacation first. Wouldn't that be fun?"

"Oh, Sam. Pa'll have the answer. I know he will." Mella's voice was full of hope.

Sam placed a kiss gently on her forehead as if wanting to hold on to that moment, a time when his Mella was herself again. He enfolded her, wishing there was an answer.

# CHAPTER
# 5

Dawn hovered like a guardian over the vacation cabin, a soft blush penetrating the curtains upstairs.

Mella shivered, quickly dressing to ward off the early morning chill. Her heart was anxious, its beating, she thought, sure to awaken her spouse and the little ones sleeping nearby. But they were too weary from travel, Sam having made the long trip with hardly a catnap.

This was Noonoon's favorite time of day, and Mella soon realized why when nature's crisp breath greeted her at the doorway. The woods smelled piney, and their wildness intensified her own expectations—surely her father would know what to do for Patty.

Mella paused for a moment on the front step, taking in the early morning sweet scent of woods and water. Birds were just calling their first notes from branches overhead.

On a rustic bench sat her father, whittling on a stick. Mella didn't want to break in on this holy hour of his, one of meditation and communion with the Creator.

"Ah, Meline! You up dis early, after so late coming?"

"I couldn't sleep any longer, Pa. Did you read my letters about Patty?" Mella asked eagerly.

The old man put the wood down and drew his daughter to the seat beside him. "I see her last night. You and Sam havta carry her all da time now?"

"Mostly. She can walk a little, but she's so uncoordinated, Pa. That's why I'm here. You've always had a cure for everything when we were young. Tell me," she pleaded, "what's the cure for Patty?"

Noonoon's gray-black mustache twitched uncomfortably. Then he sighed and took Mella's hand. He looked deep into her eyes, as if searching for her response ahead of time.

"Meline, I hava no cure for Patty. You must put her in a place with other children lika her and giva Sam and Paula your time. Hava more children! You're young."

However tender his words, they sounded heartless to Mella. "Not you, Pa! How could you, of all people, say such a thing?"

"Looka you, Meline! You so tired. Patty will get bigger and bigger, so much to care for. Little Paula needsa lotsa help too. You gonna get sick, Meline," he warned.

Mella wouldn't listen. She dropped the subject with an icy, "You want me to fix your breakfast?"

With that she went inside, keeping busy, trying to forget that her beautiful visions of Noonoon healing Patty had just turned to dust. She avoided any more talk that might threaten the leftover hope she was nourishing.

Mella felt betrayed, alone. No one seemed to understand, not even her own father who, all her life, had been sort of a human remedy. His wonder-working potions of herbs and prayer had always healed her, and when she was depressed his words had soothed her.

But now this man of Mella's fondest respect had taken a new form by repeating the unforgettable advice of the intern. Institutionalize Patty? Mella felt she would never bow to such a thing.

Her aloof air clouded the few vacation days remaining. She went about the cabin, seeming comfortable, for once, with Nonna's wordiness. An occasional "uh-huh" would suffice, but then Mella would burrow once more into her own world.

Noonoon wondered about this great change in his Meline. *How longa has Sam puta up with dis? Whatsa da cause for her unusual stubbornness? Did I, perhaps, spoil her too mucha when she was* bambina? Whatever the reason he knew she needed to bend that iron will of hers to face the inevitable. But he wisely kept quiet, leaving his daughter to learn from experience. How he wished to shield her from the coming grief.

Soon the entire family was back on Illinois Street in Detroit, and Sam had left for his new post in Great Lakes. Paula was almost 18 months and quite a handful for her mother and grandmother in the big house. The toddler's one feverish goal was to reach the top of the forbidden stairway.

Each time Nonna caught her scooting up the stairs, she would streak after her and plop the wriggling body into her playpen. But after Paula fussed awhile, Nonna would weaken and free the baby, only to find herself chasing her up the stairwell again, bellowing, to Paula's delight.

A day came, however, when she paid no heed to the toddler's complaints, and Paula was left in the pen for hours while Nonna whisked about the house busily tidying everything in sight. Carlo's future bride, Helen, was visiting that day, and the Serris would be discussing wedding plans.

The kitchen overflowed with savory aromas, and everyone appeared excited, especially Mella's only brother Carlo. A phone call sent him out the door for his intended, while Nonna remained to brood nervously. The old woman sat knotting her handkerchief, scrutinizing the couch where Patty lay drooling, making happy sounds, not really words anymore. Suddenly, Nonna jumped up and began to cart the child up the stairs.

Mella stopped her. "What are you doing with Patty, Ma?"

"Oh, Meline, I must hide her. We don'ta want Helen to tink her children will be lika Patty."

All the months of bitterness swelled inside Mella, giving way to hot, furious tears. Mella couldn't take this, what she thought an insult to her little girl. In her haste and anger she never considered her mother's background. All Mella saw was the shame in the old woman's face, a look that would fester and hurt for days.

Nonna made matters worse by explaining, "It's all right, Meline. I keep little Paula down here for Helen to see—"

"Forget it!" Mella blasted, grabbing Patty and leaving poor Nonna perplexed, wondering what she had said to cause such an outburst.

Within the hour Mella was packed and had moved in with her sister, Tina. When Helen met the Baileys later, how she loved Patty. Certainly, Nonna had misjudged this newest family member. Nonna was caught in an ancient darkness that surrounded disorders like Patty's. The old woman had her own potpourri of blame for Patty's illness, foolish smatterings of folklore and neighborhood gossip about sailors and mixed marriage.

At Tina and Remo's, the Baileys were welcome. But Mella easily read the look on her eldest sister's face, and could understand her agony. After all, the spry, chubby toddler who had left for Norfolk a few years before, had returned a spastic invalid. Tina, who had shared life's blows with her youngest sister over the years, felt this one keenly. Adding to it was Mella's own sad disposition, almost too much for Tina to bear. So when Sam found a place of their own on Kirby Street, Mella was thankful.

It was January and bitter cold, but the small rental was snug and warm, and close to the streetcar route.

As a special surprise for Sam, one day Mella decided to have studio pictures taken of his two "gals." With the appointment made, she dressed Patty and Paula meticulously, then bundled them for a cold walk to the trolley stop. Snow blanketed the ground as the baby trudged beside Mella, who carried Patty.

When they finally entered an impressive-looking building, Mella sighed, knowing the destination was near when she could rest her weary arms.

Outside the elevator she overheard a lady whispering behind her, "Hmph! Look at that—carrying the big one and making the poor little one walk!"

Mella whirled around and snapped at the woman, "My daughter's an invalid. Don't you think I'd let her walk if she could?" Later when Mella sat in the studio, remorse crept over her. For the first time since the awful onset, she took an objective look at herself. *Is this really me? What's happened to the loving person I used to be?* The reflection was short-lived but a beginning, something to draw her out of the world in which she had shut herself and her sweet child.

Through an acquaintance, Mella found a doctor who wanted to experiment on Patty with antigen shots. So, twice a week Mella made the trip to his office for the injections, then watched hopefully for improvement. None came. As time went by Patty lost control of her bladder and needed diapers again. Day by day Mella's workload was increasing.

One afternoon she stopped by her parents' house and Nonna introduced her to a visitor, a tall, slender woman, her unpainted face looking freshly scrubbed, and eager for whatever came her way.

The visitor greeted Mella's girls cheerfully. "So this is Patty—and Paula! I've heard lots about you."

In little time the two women were wrapped in hearty conversation, with Nonna passively listening in as she bounced between the couch and kitchen.

Mella surprised herself by unburdening to the stranger. And before long, the visitor knew Patty's tragic story, from the horrible nights of screaming to the university doctor's ultimatum. The visitor also sensed the gloom and guilt enshrouding the mother before her.

"Mella," she began, hesitantly at first, "deep down inside, are you blaming God for Patty's illness?"

"Well," Mella said, eyeing Nonna who was heading again to the broth on the stove, "I suppose I probably do blame God in a way. When I pray I ask Him 'Why? Why have You allowed this to happen to my beautiful daughter?' "

The visitor thought for a moment and said, "I know your father well. What if he had been the one who had caused Patty to get sick? How would you feel toward him?"

Mella brushed her hand across her daughter's pale cheek. "Angry," she replied bluntly.

"And could you still love your father, knowing he had

harmed Patty that way? Could you still serve him as a good daughter should?"

Mella lowered her eyes. "It would be very hard. But Pa wouldn't hurt a gnat. He's a loving person.

"Of course!" The visitor chuckled softly. "And our Father God is millions of times more loving than your Pa."

"Yeah?" Mella challenged. "If He's so loving, then how could he let this awful thing happen to my Patty?"

"Ah, but Mella, there's another power at work in this world, a power trying to get people to blame God for all the evil that happens to us."

"You mean—Satan?"

The woman nodded. "God isn't some big monster; He's not the one responsible for all the pain in the world. Satan is. You see, in a way, God has been forced to allow bad things to happen to good people in order to reveal Satan's true self—and the dreadful results of sin."

Seeing Mella's puzzled look she explained further. "Someday when the end comes, there will be no doubts about Satan and sin. Only the record will remain and your sweet Patty will be a part of that record. All the other innocent people hurt or killed throughout history will also be in those books. Then, when we, God's followers, examine all the evidence—including the nail-scarred hands of Jesus—we'll hate sin and its hideous results so much we'll never want to sin again—ever!" She shook her head. "No more Lucifers will rise up against God."

Mella was silent a moment, then asked, "Why didn't God just destroy Lucifer in the first place, so none of these awful things would happen?"

"Because then we would serve God out of fear instead of love. God wants us to love Him of our own free will. You can't force love, you know. He wants us to learn what a loving, gentle Father He is."

"That's beautiful," Mella sighed, "but how do you know these things?"

The woman smiled. "Because of studying books such as Job, Romans, and Revelation in the Bible. Believe me, Mella, our loving Father in Heaven doesn't go around smiting innocent children with dreadful diseases. It hurts Him deeply to see you suffer this way."

"Then why doesn't He heal Patty?"

"I don't have all the answers," the visitor admitted. "But I do think God sometimes allows hardships for certain reasons. For one thing hardships make our characters stronger. Someday you'll look back and realize that."

Mella thought, *Me strong? Nothing could be further from the truth.*

The unusual conversation stayed with Mella a long time, serving as a refreshing reminder of one bright afternoon when she was able to wander briefly from despondency.

Mella continued to keep busy during the daytime, but after her girls were bedded down in the evenings, she would feel an emptiness without her Sam. All week she looked forward to Friday night when he would burst through the doorway with, "How's my gals?" Just that phrase lifted her spirits. Sam chased away the weekday doldrums, and they would all delight in one another's company for two laughter-filled days.

One such weekend Mella shared the news about a monastery where a monk had supposedly performed many miracles. "Do you think I should take Patty, Sam?"

Her husband bit his lip. He was remembering the doctors' advice. "I don't see why you shouldn't. Only, Mella, please don't get your hopes up again."

"I won't."

Monday morning Mella left Paula with her aunt Tina and took Patty to see the so-called miracle-worker.

Following a heavyset monk, Mella made her way through a long, hollow-sounding corridor, to a room where another mother waited. Her face bore Mella's same anxious look. She was seeking prayer for her 6-year-old son who had been hit by a swing, resulting in brain damage.

Soon this woman was having an audience with the monk. Mella sent up a quick, but fervent, prayer for the pitiful boy, as well as for her own daughter.

She could hear muffled tones of the monk's voice and thought she heard him say "chiropractor."

Feeling a cool exhilaration when her turn came, Mella carried Patty into the office. The monk's smile was pleasant, putting her at ease until Patty let out a cry and raised her hand to the priest.

Happy tears rolled down Mella's cheeks. Patty hadn't raised her hand like that for over a year! Could it be that her daughter was responding to something truly miraculous in this man? Then, resting his hand gently on Patty's blonde head, he bowed and softly prayed for the child.

Turning to Mella he said, "There's nothing wrong with her. Take her to a chiropractor." The words seemed contradictory to the prayer, but Mella followed his instructions.

She set up an appointment with a girlfriend's father who was a chiropractor specializing in cranial technique. After initial X-rays, Mella kept the weekly appointments with him, as well as the twice-weekly ones for antigen injections. But neither therapy appeared to be helping Patty. She was completely spastic by this time, unable to control her motions, her legs and arms dwindling to skin and bone. Still, Mella clung to the hope that somewhere a therapy or miracle waited to unlock the door to her daughter's recovery.

Near the end of winter Mella's evenings of solitude were intensified with new worry. Patty began to experience periods of odd breathing that sometimes lasted several hours.

"Oh, God, don't let her die!" she prayed desperately.

During one of these episodes Sam's Bible on the bed stand seemed to beckon to her. She thumbed through it, finding the twenty-third psalm. The words gave her such comfort that she knew they had been written just for her. She marked the page, never realizing the many times she would call upon those same phrases for consolation.

Closing the book, she went back to her child's bedside, her heart beating time to, "Yea, though I walk through the valley of the shadow of death, I will fear no evil: for thou art with me."

Spring arrived with another birthday, the third for Patty.

Then her father came home with the announcement, "I have orders for San Diego!"

It was in that city on the waterfront that Sam and Mella had met and fallen in love. He thought perhaps the move would recapture some of his wife's old self, the happy girl of a few short years before.

But her immediate reaction was negative. "Move all the way out there away from our families? How could we?"

Sam assured her that he had tried to get a hardship change, but the Navy had said in so many words, "Go or get out of the service."

Not long after that Mella heard of a special clinic in Ann Arbor, Michigan, for children like Patty. When she set up an appointment, a lost radiance showed in her tired face.

*Maybe . . . just maybe . . .* Again she was hoping for a miracle. *I'll ask my brother for his car.*

Telling her parents about the clinic, she was surprised by Noonoon's reply, "I go witha you, Meline. Tina'll taka care of da *bambina.*"

Mella smiled in agreement, thinking perhaps she had misjudged her father. Maybe he wasn't as callous about Patty's condition as she had supposed.

Morning was still dark when the sleepy threesome started out of the city toward Ann Arbor. Heavy-laden clouds hung low over the highway as if predicting the tears that would fall by day's end.

The hours passed slowly at the clinic. Test after test for Patty were preceded by tedious question-and-answer sessions for her mother. All the while Noonoon remained at Mella's side, determined to be there for the verdict. He intuitively sensed a bad report and expected his Meline to come to grips with the truth. He prayed for her to face it squarely this time, not to hide from it any longer. And he prayed, in his own touching vernacular, for "da hurt not ta break her ta pieces."

Finally, a young, good-looking doctor addressed Mella, his voice fully sympathetic. "Mrs. Bailey, from all the information we've gathered here, it looks like your daughter has a form of cerebral palsy. There's a possibility that the brain damage occurred at the time of her smallpox vaccination, causing post-vaccination encephalitis."

"And the treatment for this palsy?" Mella asked naively.

The physician looked sober, shaking his head. "I'm sorry. There's no known treatment for this condition. There's nothing we can do for her."

Bitter words escaped Mella. "Why do they give children the vaccinations then?" Her rude tone made her father cringe. He seemed to be bracing himself for a storm.

"It's better for one to react unfavorably than to have all come down with the killer disease, Mrs. Bailey."

Minutes later, Noonoon lifted Patty into the waiting car, covering her frail arms lovingly, saying nothing. The patient lines around his eyes now had a stony sadness about them.

Mella stared at the sleeping child. *No known treatment.* The phrase sliced its way through her mind, opening old wounds. Hard, cold facts fell upon her as she stood face to face with the real Patty, a hopeless victim of a medical quirk. She saw her child for who she was, for who she could never be. Never to run, never to chatter and share her girlish secrets, never to fall in love, never to do anything but lie passively through life.

Mella, silently taking her place in the driver's seat, became lost in thought. *How could I have been so stupid to hope again? I should have known better . . . Why my child? Why my beautiful Patty?*

Then a great ache seized her heart and tears rained down upon the steering wheel. A black sky was crying with her, and the desolate countryside passing by seemed to share her mood. Quaint bridges along the roadway went unnoticed until Mella reached her lowest ebb. *If Pa wasn't in this car, I could run off the road. Just Patty and me. Sam would take care of Paula . . .*

But her father was there, suffering with his daughter—in silence, a silence she needed. No words could comfort just then. The bleak future stretched itself drearily before her, but Noonoon's strength seemed to penetrate the air, giving Mella a share, to help her go on with her child.

# CHAPTER

# 6

Traveling east along El Cajon Boulevard, Sam and Mella made a merry duet. Although she sang alone, her husband's sparkling eyes were as good as music. He had found a house, and all he needed was her approval.

Three-year-old Patty was resting on her mother's lap, and Paula was enjoying the balmy mixture of song and late-afternoon sunshine.

Sam loved this country, perhaps because it reminded him of Texas—not that the land was flat, but that the California hills were virtually treeless, the earth parched and weeded, ruffled only by an occasional whirlwind. A few adobe dwellings, set down in beds of sagebrush, seemed to reach far back into their Spanish past.

Simply the fact that San Diego was where Sam had wooed his bride in the first place must have encouraged him. Whatever the reason, his love for the country was apparent in his every glance.

Despite the contrast to Detroit's bustling, crowded streets, Mella, too, found herself enchanted with the desolate beauty, a sweet reminder of their courtship days.

Nearing their destination, they felt overwhelmed by a hueless presence off to the left. A giant mountain followed them until they turned right onto Highland Drive and headed down to the corner of Chatham Street.

"Here we are!" Sam announced. "I think there are only

about 10 other houses in this new community called Fletcher Hills. We'd be kind of like pioneers. That is if you approve, of course."

Mella began to survey the yard of bald earth, then the light blue, concrete walls that formed the rectangular house. A brick flower bed around the front porch greeted them at the entrance.

"Geraniums would look pretty there," she declared, not really committing herself.

Sam carried Patty into the living room, his wife following, easing Paula down to the floor to run through the vacant rooms.

"Oooo! It's cool in here, Sam."

"Sure is, hon! Kind of reminds you of a bomb shelter, doesn't it?"

Mella winced at the comparison as Sam continued. "The flat roof, walls, floors, everything is concrete. Best insulation!"

Mella followed the brown floor tiles into the kitchen to the right and back into the area adjacent to the living room.

"What's this?"

"Well, it could be the dining room or a bedroom," Sam replied, demonstrating how the accordion-style divider worked.

The east wall was made up of linen and clothes closets, while the south part had a large picture window looking out over Fletcher Hills toward Mount Helix.

After inspecting the bath and two bedrooms, Mella and Sam strolled out the back door. The spacious yard, a triangle of broken ground, lay before a gully that separated the property from a two-story on Highland. A few eucalyptus trees, tall and spindly, bordered the street.

"And Mella, come and see the garage! It has a sink. Maybe eventually we'll get you a washing machine."

"And you could put up a clothesline here and a large trellis for roses there and another trellis on that side of the house and—"

"Wait a minute, gal!" Sam interrupted. "You've got me

doing all this work already and haven't told me—should we buy the house?"

"Of course! I love it."

Soon Mella was gathering Paula's small self into her arms and joining her spouse at the car for a drive through their new neighborhood.

A few front yards already had lawns, giving the street a homey look. At the top of Highland they turned east. The road dropped quickly, revealing El Cajon Valley.

"Oh, Sam!" Mella breathed.

The small city beckoned with its valley of twinkling lights adding wonder to the townscape. The Laguna Mountains in the distance bordered a vast ridge, their faded hues bidding farewell to the day.

The Baileys traveled a few miles more while Mella "ooed" and "ahed" at the surroundings. The Ford turned facing a sunset of crimson and peach along the western skyline. The couple quietly marveled at the scene until Mella whispered, "Sam, let's go by our house once more before we leave."

They drove slowly by the darkened walls, Mella gazing beyond them toward Mount Helix.

"Look! What's that?" Mella was delighted to see an illuminated cross at the top of the mountain. Her kitchen and dining room windows faced it. *Seems like a good omen*, she thought, resting against the seat.

Patty's hair framed her sleeping face as Mella cuddled her close. The child looked normal when sleeping, no different from Paula, also snoozing, in the back seat. But Mella knew as soon as Patty woke, her spastic mouth would begin to drool, her still, slender arms would fling about uncontrollably, and her legs would barely support her own weight.

As Mella gazed tenderly at the stricken girl, her eyes filled with hope. Maybe this new home would be a special kind of sanctuary for them, a place where people would accept Patty. And somehow the thought always returned. *Maybe it will be the place where Patty will be cured and run around the house just as Paula did a few hours ago.*

The sky grayed quickly, but Mella was unaware of the coming blackness. She was eyeing the few stars already aglow that seemed to symbolize a turning in her life, one of happier tomorrows.

The Bailey family was eager to move from their temporary housing in National City. The air had a sweet expectancy that even the little ones felt. But, one afternoon the mood changed abruptly when Patty, who had been propped up with pillows on the bed, somehow got by her guards and fell between the bed and wall.

Mella gasped, realizing what the crashing sound was, fully expecting a commotion. Strangely, though, her daughter didn't utter a sound.

After struggling with the large poster bed, Mella screamed, "Sam! Patty's choking!"

He came at once, sweeping Patty into his arms and laying her across the bed.

"Mella, get my wallet! Looks like a seizure!"

He began undoing Patty's dress sash, then tried to take her pulse. Patty's arms, however, were flailing stiffly before her, so Sam gave up. Just keeping her from harming herself with this sudden brute strength was enough.

Patty's face muscles were constricted like the rest of her body, her eyes had rolled back into her head, and except for the movement, she looked like death itself.

"Oh, God—please!" was all that Mella could muster as she stood watching Sam who seemed unusually calm.

"This is strange, Mella. She's not biting down like in a seizure. We don't need the wallet after all." A few seconds later he added, "I think she's coming out of it now, honey. See? Her muscles are relaxing."

Although the convulsion had passed, Patty's eyes were glassed over and had the same faraway look Mella had first noticed in Norfolk. But soon Patty fell into a deep sleep.

Mella and Sam were unaware of the lifelong series of convulsions that would follow this first one. Drugs curbed them somewhat, but at times the spasms were frequent, and Mella learned to care for Patty without becoming overwrought, taking the episodes in stride.

Because they were one of few families in the new community of Fletcher Hills, their home seemed isolated at first, a felt difference from the populous housing units of before. And Mella found herself with second thoughts about their dream bungalow. But by February most of their neighbors had arrived, making up for the few months of solitude.

One day Mella was studying her primitive living room setting. Lots of sunshine poured through the drapeless windows, spotlighting the few orange crates and Patty's cot, the only furnishings.

*Well, at least we have the table and chairs here in the kitchen. I'm thankful for that*, Mella thought while fumbling through some clutter for a two-quart container.

"Here's the punch!" next-door neighbor, Donna, announced through an open window. She held up a filled pitcher.

As if planned, two other women knocked at the back door, and soon the four ladies were perched at the kitchen table, sipping the refreshment and reveling in each other's company. It was discovery time, a brief unraveling of pasts to begin their newfound friendship. Once in a while, eager child faces, sunburned and freckled, appeared only to be shooed outside again.

Four of those youngsters belonged to Jo Murphy, a dainty Irisher, who didn't quite fill the crisp maternity top she was wearing. There was a competent strength in her slender arms, despite her seeming a bit shy. Her nonchalant tones denoted patience—a fortunate virtue, considering the size of her growing family. Her calm nature was quite different from Mella's, but Mella was taken with Jo at once. Here was a friend! The Murphys would be close-at-hand too, occupying the two-story across the gully.

Sometime between introductions Mella had brought Patty to the cot in the living room. She had shared only a little about the child's condition, when she realized that Patty's presence hadn't changed her company's mood. Along with a few sympathetic smiles, they had accepted her handicapped child as eagerly as the glasses of punch. Mella thrilled at the thought of such acceptance.

Jo's next-door neighbor, Darlene Johnson, was the mother of two young girls. Darlene seemed rather saucy at first, but Mella learned quickly that under the pert exterior lay a warm, generous heart. The Dutch bob of auburn hair swished about Darlene's face as she excused herself from the gathering.

"If my old man gets home and finds I don't have supper ready, he'll raise the roof." Then she laughed as if it wouldn't really bother her too much if her husband did get angry.

Mrs. Johnson parted company after casting a disapproving look Paula's way. Little did the youngster know that the slim woman would soon become her disciplinarian, a second mother for a while.

Donna, the nearest neighbor, remained and eventually confided, "I would love to invite you people to supper, but I never know about Earl . . ." Her voice trailed off. She was searching Mella's face, wondering if she should share a confidence so soon.

Her husband was an alcoholic, she explained, and his latest binges were sources of grief and embarrassment to her as well as their two young sons.

Mella assured Donna that she understood and appreciated her thoughtfulness.

Waving goodbye Mella found herself alone, sitting in the calm, her eyes wet with happiness as she realized her dream of acceptance was coming true. The years of disappointment and bitterness were melting away and, for a time, forgotten. Now only gladness was there, like a healing tide washing away all the anguish. Her new friends made her feel she had truly come home at last.

# 7

As days turned to weeks, the neighborhood punch gatherings continued, times precious to Mella when she could sit and enjoy fellowship and, at the same time, rest. Patty and Paula both were growing, and so was Mella's burden. By mid-afternoon her back would become one throbbing ache.

But when mornings were fresh, Mella's hopes were high. She would make up a long list of the day's chores and tack it to the wall.

Laundry time at the Bailey's was no secret. From the moment the washing machine started to the last clothespin on the line, Mella sang. She bellowed out medleys curiously composed from her Italian collection, as well as western ballads and Protestant hymns Sam had taught her.

Meanwhile neighbors caught on, and mysterious things began to happen.

Since Mella's whereabouts were obvious when she sang, it was an excellent time for Donna or another neighbor to steal past her and look at the list. Whatever was next, whether changing Patty, folding diapers, or washing dishes, the neighbor would do it. This continued for some time before Mella caught Donna with hands in the dishwater.

At first Mella was reluctant to accept their help. But Donna made her understand that they were receiving just as much pleasure as she was, perhaps more.

"Besides," Donna argued, "coming over here and just

looking at that list makes me realize how light my burden is."

Mella sighed, but grinned her approval. How generous these women were; women with their own households to keep, but willing to share her workload.

Mella always attacked her chores with gusto, but there came a time when feeding Patty became sheer drudgery.

Day after day she would secure the girl in her high chair and begin the endless coaxing, "Come on, sweetheart! Eat for Mommy."

After the first two spoonsful Patty would balk. Paula had long since shoveled down her dinner and was out of the room before her sister would be a quarter of the way through her meal.

With the unfinished list taunting her, Mella would grow more nervous while Patty became more reluctant.

Then one lunchtime when Mella had reached the end of her patience, along came an angel in the form of Cynthia Prince. Although Cynthia was a naval officer's wife, the usual caste system didn't exist as far as she was concerned. Her affection for Patty was warm and genuine.

After observing Mella's efforts awhile, Cynthia offered, "Mind if I try?"

"No. Go right ahead! Just don't expect much."

The neighbor's voice crooned, "Now, Patty, you're going to eat for Aunt Cynthia, aren't you?"

Patty's eyes lit up, her mouth flew open, and she purred through the entire meal. Mella was grateful, but dumbfounded. She had never before witnessed such a transformation in her daughter's eating habits. Apparently, there was something unique about the newcomer's voice that worked a special charm on Patty. From then on Cynthia scheduled her visits around mealtime so she could relieve Mella of the feeding task. Mella was learning to accept these gifts of time, but secretly she wished for some way to repay the kindness.

Her wish was granted soon when three brawny men drove up and placed a telephone booth directly across the street from the Bailey home. Because all the houses in the new community were without phones, a regular communications center emerged in which Mella Bailey became the chief part.

The short Italian woman could be seen, day or night, trudging happily along roadways or through yards, her smoke-black hair swaying with her brisk pace. She felt a real sense of belonging, part of a network of lives that made her own feel fulfilled. Somehow her troubles weren't so bad, Mella thought, as she became involved more intimately with others.

And there weren't just 11 houses anymore. Cement trucks roared past the Bailey place daily as more and more homes took shape down Highland and Chatham streets. Soon the hill between the homes and El Cajon Valley became populated, doing away with the refuge for coyotes and skunks who had sometimes found their way into trash cans at night.

When Darlene Johnson felt her friendship with Mella was secure she decided to take on an unpleasant task. One day, while Paula was thrashing around on the floor in a boisterous display of temper, Darlene asked Mella if she realized what a dreadful person the child would become if her unruly ways weren't checked while she was still young.

In fact, her very words were, "Mella, society isn't going to put up with a brat like that."

Although the blunt statement stung Mella, she admitted it was true. "But I feel so guilty, Darlene. I hate to spank Paula when the poor little girl doesn't get even half the attention Patty does."

"I know, Mella. But you're doing her harm by not disciplining her. Look at that! What she needs is a good paddling to show her that a tantrum is not proper behavior."

With noticeable dread Mella consented to the punishment, but she didn't have the courage to administer it herself.

So Darlene Johnson was the one who gave Paula her first spanking. It was the dawning of a whole new way of life for the little girl.

Mella cried with Paula, but she knew the spanking was needed. From then on, when Darlene was around she took over as substitute mom, teaching Paula her "pleases" and "thank yous." And soon Mella added discipline of her own until Paula became a fairly civilized child.

During one of her phone errands Mella met a new resident—a woman with two little ones. Instead of lingering to chat as she often did, Mella invited the woman home, explaining that Donna, who was with Patty and Paula, needed to get back to her own duties.

After a brief introduction and thanks to Donna on the doorstep, Mella led the newcomer into her living room where Patty was propped in the old wicker rocker.

"Aaah!" came a noise from Patty, her greeting to them.

As Mella reached for a tissue to wipe her daughter's chin, she heard the woman behind her, the friendliness suddenly drained from her voice, "Ew! What is that?"

Mella's body stiffened. Blood rushed to her face in anger. Ordinarily, Mella would have flared up with a biting reproof. But she was a different person now. Time and good people had brought a measure of tolerance. So she took a deep breath to calm herself.

"This is Patty, my daughter. She's a victim of cerebral palsy."

The woman's disgust was evident in the words that followed. "How can you stand having that child in the house?"

It was a mocking snobbery, almost too much for Mella. Fighting her tears, Mella choked out, "Because I love her."

The reply flowed smoothly, but inside Mella's heart cried. She wanted to shout, "What's the matter with you? Can't you see how beautiful my child is? Look at the light in her eyes! Few children, even normal ones, have that kind of glow. And Patty's not a *that*. She's a human being with purpose."

But Mella held back thinking that perhaps one day young Patty would show the woman her rare quality, touch the woman's heart, and melt her prejudice.

And it happened. Within two weeks the same lady was bringing Patty gifts, sitting with her, talking to her endlessly, and most surprising of all, she was reaching for the proverbial tissue box to wipe the child's moist chin. That gesture alone was enough to erase the ill beginning as Mella watched from the doorway with tears in her eyes.

With Southern California's balmy climate came a host of flowers to brighten the yard. As promised, Sam had built trellises, and now honeysuckle vines were climbing alongside the house. Pink roses formed an entire wall of giant blossoms along the west end of the newly poured patio. Each evening the sweet smell of jasmine would fill the Bailey house.

It was the rustling of a jasmine bush one morning that prompted Mella to investigate. Thinking a dog might be damaging her flower bed, she grabbed her broom and rounded the corner, ready to oust the intruder. She was surprised to find a white-haired lad, about four years old, peeking in the window.

Mella smiled. "Hi, honey! Whatcha looking for?"

A bit bashfully the boy answered, "I heard dar was a crazy girl in dar, and I wanna see 'er."

There it was again, brazen and cutting, now through the lips of a child.

Hardly ruffled this time, Mella took the boy's hand, deliberately sugaring her response. "Well, then, come and meet Patty. But you'll find she's not crazy, dear. She just has a condition called cerebral palsy."

And so the child met Patricia Bailey and soon grew to love her just as many other neighborhood youngsters did. Without fail, she responded to them all, smiling broadly and uttering wordless exclamations that only the little ones could interpret.

Mella had seemed to inherit her father's love for mornings. Her place at the kitchen table was like an arena amidst sparrows and scenes of sleepy children straggling past to the bus stop.

One morning while Mella sat dreamily in her place, taking in the sounds of life around her, Donna, her next-door neighbor, appeared with bleary eyes.

"Oh, Mella! I'm so happy."

Fixing Donna a cup of cocoa, Mella listened while the neighbor explained, "Earl's taken the step—he's joined Alcoholics Anonymous."

Mella beamed, hugging the woman. Then dropping her

arms abruptly she asked, "But why do you look so tired?"

"When Earl returned home after the meeting last night, he felt overwhelmed. He wanted a drink so badly. Then he called his A.A. friends. Mella, they were at our house until 3:00 this morning. Can you imagine? I was in the bedroom, but I could hear them talking to Earl, struggling with him—even praying! It was beautiful, especially when you realize those men had jobs to go to this morning."

"But what made Earl decide to take the step?" Mella questioned, recalling all the times the man had promised to join A.A. before.

"You know, I've been thinking about that most of the night," Donna replied, "and as hard as it is to admit it, I think it was because of a change in me."

Tears flowed freely down Donna's face as she confessed, "It took a change in my attitude, in my dealing with Earl. I actually believe my own ways, nagging and all, contributed to his drinking problem." She paused a moment, sipping more cocoa. "I used to resent him so and was filled with such bitterness. But Mella, when I met you and realized how small my burden was compared to the one you have with Patty, my attitude changed. There was a new harmony in our home. I'm there to strengthen Earl now, not to tear him down.

"I admitted that to my husband this morning," she continued, "and although he never once blamed me, there was a closeness between us that we've never known. I just can't express how I feel."

"I think I understand." Mella blew her nose. "I'm so happy for you, Donna, and for your family."

While Mella watched her neighbor cross the yard, she thought, *What a marvelous way to start my day.*

That was only the beginning in Earl's battle with alcoholism. But after many times of strange cars parking in his driveway, Earl would be ready to take his place as counselor to other people.

Patty hadn't awakened yet, but Mella found herself by the child's bedside, gazing at her little missionary in pajamas. "Well, honey, you've done it again!"

# 8

In the spring of 1948, Sam was temporarily stationed on the U.S.S. *Seminole*. Routine took a back seat during those months when his household revolved around the ship's unpredictable homecomings. At odd intervals all four Baileys would migrate down to San Diego harbor for the farewell.

After the youngsters were properly squeezed, Mella would kiss her sailor fervently, but never with a detaining hug. She knew his passion for the sea and how he thrived on the hubbub of sick bay.

Sam, perceiving the sorrow in her dark eyes, would console her with, "I'll be back before ya know it, hon!"

One last "I love you," and up the gangplank he would trudge—again.

Mella and the girls would stay to watch the tugboats guide the giant vessel out of port until the sailors on deck were just a blur.

With deliberate cheer Mella resisted that first ache of parting. All the way home she sang at the top of her lungs, and by the time she had parked in her driveway, she was her happy self. She'd go back to her job as homemaker and message bearer, never knowing when the call would be hers, sending her and the children again to the harbor.

Days were usually full but at night, after the girls were in bed, Mella would wash dishes and stare moodily out the window at the quiet dark. The cross atop Mount Helix reminded her to pray, and occasionally, a tear mingled with her dishwater.

Then, if Paula was still awake, Mella would carry her outside to the old wicker chair that passed seasonably between living room and front porch. And there, surrounded by the sound of a soft lullaby and the delicate scent of jasmine, Paula would fall asleep.

Probably the biggest encouragement for Mella was Patty's reaction to Sam's homecoming. As soon as the girl spotted him she would cry out, her ardent gaze bounding with his down the gangplank.

Patty was always first into her father's arms, where she must have tried to voice her feelings, but only happy, meaningless syllables came out. Love was there, though, obvious and unrestrained.

After one of Sam's longest spells out at sea, the call finally came. Every part of Mella was alive with expectation as the three Baileys waited happily on the dock.

A ship arrived, sailors met loved ones, and Mella heard bits of conversations as happy couples strolled by. Two more vessels came in, but not the *Seminole.* Gradually, people thinned out until the dock looked vacant.

As the sun dropped into the water and fog gathered around the three figures on the dock, Patty fell asleep in Mella's arms, and Paula had long since lost interest in her surroundings. One more ship inched its way through the fog. Mella's eyes strained anxiously toward the lettering on the vessel. "U.S.S. . . ." It wasn't the *Seminole,* so she sighed and headed toward the car.

"Daddy no come, Mamma?" her youngest asked.

"Daddy no come, Paula. I guess the message center made a mistake."

The fog, pocketing the lowlands home, was unusually thick that night. The girls slept undisturbed beside their mother, never knowing her anxiety as she guided the car judiciously over a disappearing roadway.

Times like these made Mella realize how much she cared for Sam, how much she missed his dimpled grin and Texan "yonders." Then she recalled the night a year before, the trip from Ann Arbor, with an invisible—but far denser—fog. She smiled, thinking how far she had come in that short while. There she sat, independent of her father and husband, coping, taking each day at a time, actually enjoying them and the precious people who had made this rebirth possible.

When Sam's seafaring days ended, he settled dutifully into his new position at San Diego Naval Hospital. Patty was 4 by then, and Paula, edging actively out of babyhood, was a meddlesome 3-year-old.

It soon became apparent that Patty's convulsions oftentimes coincided with any unusual excitement, such as birthday festivities or boisterous company. And when the spasms came, all else stopped.

Mella would sit beside the child, talk calmly to her, and struggle with the strong arms that flailed.

Although quite young, Paula still sensed the anguish these episodes caused her mother. It was then that "Please, God, make Patty get better," took on new meaning in the youngster's nightly prayers.

But there were more good times than not, when Patty's pretty, brown eyes were alive with expression—a light of cognizance that baffled even the specialists. It wasn't a dull glimmer, but a sensitive look that encouraged doctors and caused friends to help Mella in her never-ending quest to find a cure.

A friend called Mella one day, inviting her to bring Patty to a little church in the valley. An evangelist, "gifted with healing powers," she said, was holding a nightly crusade in which many had already been healed.

The old feelings, lying dormant for so long, began to flourish. Immediately, Mella was caught in a vision of Patty skipping about the house, talking, running to her, hugging her neck. Here, Mella thought, was another chance.

She found a stray dime in her apron pocket and called Sam, soon divulging her news with the enthusiasm of a child.

He responded with silence for a few moments then said,

"Sweetheart, I can't stand the thought of you being hurt again—"

"But, Sam, you believe in divine healing, don't you?"

"Of course, Mella. It's biblical, only some people are misguided and don't use—"

"Honey, please . . ." Mella's pleading voice touched Sam's heart, so with reservations, he consented.

That evening Paula was placed in Darlene Johnson's care while Sam and Mella took Patty down the hill to a small, white church. Although they arrived early, the building was already almost full. A kind-looking gentleman ushered the Baileys to a pew near the back.

Mella held Patty close while studying the simple decor. It looked so plain compared to St. Mary's where she attended—no statues, no candles, only a stark white cross in back of the rostrum.

More people filtered in, filling the remaining pews—a few men in wheelchairs, a woman on crutches—all sharing Mella's hope. As people crowded closer, the air felt clammy, and Patty began to whimper until the minister led in the singing of a lively opening hymn.

Sam and Mella bowed with the others while the pastor prayed. On and on he went, his voice rising and falling. Finally, the prayer ended and another spirited song followed, its rhythm pulsating like one large heartbeat, faster and faster, culminating in a high resounding finish. Then stillness fell on the congregation as they watched the guest speaker step to the pulpit.

"Brothers and sisters," he began. He preached loudly, his voice thundering and quivering dramatically. His hands swayed in swooping gestures as he gave examples from previous nights. Pacing back and forth on the platform, he quoted scriptures vehemently while loud amens rose from the crowd to spur him on.

Then the minister stopped mid-stage, and with out-stretched arms, summoned, "All who want healing tonight, come forward! Come forward, brothers, and sisters, ye who are heavy laden!"

The woman on crutches was the first to venture forth. Others followed. The evangelist laid his hands atop the woman's head and prayed fervently, his eyes wide open, staring at the ceiling. Up jumped the woman without her crutches.

"I can walk! I can walk!" she screamed.

An excited response rose from the onlookers. Mella, too, was stirred by this seeming miracle. While incoherent prayers and praise intensified around her, she was no longer an observer, but fast becoming a part of the mass that bristled with excitement.

Then she saw him, a man slithering like a snake down the aisle, making his way forward. She felt overcome by an urge to follow, but Sam's strong hand kept her back.

Her husband was deep in thought, recalling scriptures from his Sunday school days. *"The Spirit itself beareth witness with our spirit . . ."* and *"Let all things be done decently and in order."*

Sam's feelings were mixed. He thought the minister was relying more on his own ability than that of God. Common sense told him to leave before Patty's turn. But Sam knew that if his wife didn't have her chance, she would always wonder. When the crowd up front dispersed, Sam carried his daughter forward, with Mella at his side.

"Leave her with me, dear people!" the preacher urged. Then he stood Patty up on her feet, supported her at the shoulders, and commanded, "Satan, come out! Come out from this child!"

*Satan?* Sam's face reddened. He wondered, *Where's the name of Jesus, that should rightly be in such a command?*

When the evangelist eased his hold on Patty, her body was still limp, so he restrengthened his grip and tried again, this time calling even louder, "This child who has done no harm to anyone, stand and walk to me!"

When he let go of Patty's shoulders, her body folded downward. One of the ushers grabbed her quickly before she hit the floor. Mella's cheeks were soaked with tears. She wanted the healing so desperately. Her child had to walk and talk again. She had to!

"Please, God, please!" she begged, her hoarse voice adding to the babble around her.

One more time the man tried and failed. So he turned the child around for the congregation to gawk at. Patty's face had lost its light. She looked listless and pathetic, dangling from the man's hands like a long, fragile puppet.

The evangelist then boomed like Job's accusers of old, "See this child, brothers and sisters! She's the result of secret sin. There's some terrible deed in the past that prevents her healing." Then turning his fiery eyes upon the parents, he thundered, "Confess it, dear people! Confess it that your child might walk!"

Sam could stand still no longer. He rushed up to the minister, swept Patty into his arms, and motioned for Mella to follow. On their way to the door they passed many wondering faces.

Mella was so upset that she cried all the way home. Sam knew it was useless to try comforting her, so he let her cry until she blurted, "What have I done? What have I done to cause Patty's sickness?"

"Oh, honey! You haven't done anything. Didn't you realize that poor man needed an excuse?" Sam reached for his wife's trembling hand. "Anyway, you've got the wrong idea about God. God is love and goodness. He didn't cause Patty's condition."

Mella was lost in thought, not really hearing what Sam was saying. They returned home to three days of misery. Patty's convulsions were almost continuous the first night. Even an increase in her medication didn't help, and in the days following she fell into a semi-stupor, hardly responding to anything.

During the whole trying time, guilt welled up in Mella, causing her to search her past for a reason for Patty's condition, a guilt that would haunt her for months.

# 9

Mella put down the pan with a deliberate thud, then she opened a cabinet, staring idly up at its cluttered shelves. *Who does that little woman think she is anyhow?* Mella thought about her newest house guest. *Running out like that, shutting herself in the bedroom again, leaving Cynthia perplexed in the doorway.*

Mella turned an embarrassed face toward Cynthia who was already feeding Patty with the usual ease. How kind she was! Such a contrast to the miniature cyclone that had just breezed through.

Well, this was the final blow. Mella would have to confront Juanita now, fix that antisocial way of hers before it turned the house into a regular hermit's shack.

Ever since the night Sam brought home the Gillams to live until they found a place of their own, the Bailey haven was far from peaceful.

Ted was big, easy-going, and friendly enough, but his wife was another story. Shyness, Mella guessed, kept Juanita in her room all day, barely venturing forth for meals. Then when visitors stopped by, Juanita's mute scurry out of their presence ruffled more than a few feathers. This latest incident fired Mella with the spunk to retaliate—tactfully, she hoped.

Laying her dishtowel aside, she smiled an "excuse me" at Cynthia, then marched through the hallway.

"Juanita, may I come in?"

Mella opened the door. There sat the Texan, looking small on the roll-away bed, her face expressionless. It was that blank stare that baffled Mella. Her Italian temperament rallied around emotion, and she prided herself in being sensitive to other's needs. But this girl was different.

Juanita was beautiful. No one could deny that. Her soft, green eyes, her nose and lips—all arranged just so—made more than one man glance her way, especially when she wore her trim Wave's uniform.

Mella's mood changed when she studied Juanita's face. *She's a young kid, maybe just scared,* she thought.

Mella recalled seeing a hint of compassion in those same green eyes the night before when a stray cat had wandered to their doorstep. Juanita eagerly took in the creature, fed him, and stroked his fur until midnight. Mella also remembered that same look being cast Patty's way once.

She chose her words carefully. "My house has always been one of love, Juanita. I can't have you turning it into something else. People won't want to come here anymore."

"I—I—just don't feel at ease around strangers." A drawl barely escaped her curt reply. Then Juanita sat silent, pretending not to care. She would be glad when Ted found their own place. She wouldn't have to impose on Sam's wife any longer, wouldn't have to be in the midst of such bedlam—people in and out all day long, children everywhere, women taking over chores like they lived there. Her barracks in the service hadn't been so chaotic.

Mella continued, "They wouldn't be strangers long, young lady, if you'd stick around and get to know them. They're warm, generous people, Juanita." Then she added the challenge, "Are you afraid to try?"

"No."

Her short answer told Mella nothing. Was she failing to reach her? Once more Mella urged, "Your lunch is getting cold, hon. Come on out and eat it. You don't have to say much. Just try, OK?"

"Is that—that captain's wife still there?"

"Yes, but you'll find her as ordinary as a plain ol' enlisted man's mate."

Juanita doubted that, but followed half-heartedly to the kitchen. After all, she *was* hungry.

That was the beginning. Although Juanita remained aloof at first, she came to know Donna, Jo Murphy and her tribe, and Darlene Johnson. Easing into their lives, Juanita found herself adjusting to the hubbub of the Bailey household, that strangely enough, did have a semblance of order—at least in Mella's proverbial list hanging center-stage.

Mella had rightly perceived Juanita's love for Patty. No longer afraid to show that affection, Juanita would rock the child and sing to her by the hour.

One day her sweet voice chanted, "One-alar, two-alar, sack-alar, sand . . ." and Paula wandered in.

"Whatcha singin', Aunt Juanita? Teach me!"

"I will," she promised, "but right now I'm teaching Patty." With that, the child she rocked purred like the kitten Juanita had held a week earlier.

The other strays Juanita would bring home were an odd composite, everyone from a lonely old man found in a park to an entire family of carnival people. Mella became used to these visitors and welcomed them in the same way she welcomed the homeless sailors Sam brought home.

Mella grew to love Juanita like a sister. In fact, the Gillams had been informally adopted with Paula adding "Uncle" and "Aunt" to their names. When Juanita and Ted did find their own place, they remained a part of the Bailey family, often showing up for meals and going on outings with them.

May brought brighter, warmer days, more flowers, sprinklers watering lawns—and children. Although the season's change wasn't as pronounced as back East, Mella still felt the rebirth all about her.

The old phone booth had done its duty. Lines threaded their way to homes now, so the message center was a thing of the past. But the friendships formed during those one-telephone years would endure for Mella.

One morning, when Mella stood gazing out at the cross glistening in the sunshine, her phone rang.

Patty and Paula were in the living room, out of Mella's sight while she talked. Suddenly, Patty went into a convulsion. Since Paula had watched her mother many times, in her 4-year-old mind she knew she could do what her mother would do. After all, she was a "big girl" now.

So Paula took hold of her sister's arms, and with all her childish might fought against Patty's strength. Calmly Paula told her sister, "It's all right, Patty. Everything is going to be OK. Paula's here . . ."

Mella gasped as she rounded the corner. "What are you doing?" There was a terror in her eyes Paula had never seen before.

"I'm just copying you, Mommy. Patty's having a spasm."

Quickly, Mella took over, moving the youngster out of the way. "Why didn't you call me?"

"You were on the phone, Mommy. I didn't want to bother you." Paula felt angry. *Why was Mommy so worried? I was doing just fine with Patty.*

After the convulsion subsided and Patty lay still, not quite asleep, Mella took Paula into the kitchen and sat her down.

"Paula, I know you think you were helping Patty, and you were, except that she could hurt you."

"Oh, no!" Paula argued. "Mommy, Patty would never hurt me. She loves me."

Tears teased at Mella's eyes. "I know she does, darling, but when Patty has a convulsion she gets very strong. Paula, her arms could— could—" Mella sighed. "They could hurt you very badly. You must always call Mama. Promise me you will."

"OK, I promise," the girl muttered, wishing she were older. Then her mom wouldn't have to go through those trying times. She knew the anxiety the spasms caused, and she wanted to protect her mother from them.

The phone call had been about a school for handicapped children, soon opening near Campo. Mella had dismissed the notion of boarding Patty until she saw Paula with her.

Now her thoughts raced. *Maybe the school could help. Maybe Patty could learn to use her hands. But it's so far away. How would I ever bear the separation? And I couldn't possibly make the visits to Campo by myself.* The school was near the Mexican border, and there were acres of wilderness between El Cajon and there.

As Mella later voiced these objections, Sam answered each, then suggested they might at least speak to the director. If Mella didn't like the place, they could dismiss the idea.

That week the four Baileys journeyed toward Campo. Along the way Mella's dread grew. She could hear her father's voice, *"You must put her in a place with other children lika her and giva Sam and Paula your time."* How could she? Was she giving up too easily, shirking her responsibility? Maybe she was the only one who could ever really care for her daughter.

Several times Mella wanted Sam to turn the car around, to forget the venture, but he encouraged, "Remember, if you don't like the place—"

"I know. I know."

Sam felt sorry for his wife, but knew her burden all too well. Patty's delicate frame had narrowed. She was not only lean, but tall now, and this extra weight added more time to her daily care. Sam wished that Mella could get some rest, even for a few months. He knew it would do her good.

When they finally reached the few buildings nestled into a hillside, the school looked inviting. In fact, it seemed to be an oasis compared to the wilderness through which they had just traveled, and Mella's face brightened.

The director was also encouraging, her sincerity real. She was an older woman with high hopes for her school, and painted lovely pictures of children using their hands and beginning the rudiments of caring for themselves. Although the expense would take a big chunk out of their budget, the Baileys were impressed.

It was decided. They would take Patty, her crib, and her belongings to the school the following week for a trial stay.

When the time came to leave Patty, Mella agonized. This

was her own daughter she was leaving behind, the girl who had filled the largest part of her life for five years.

Sunshine flooded the spacious room where Patty lay in her crib. But Mella's spirits were dark as she kissed her, looking into the big, brown eyes that didn't understand the goodbye. The light was there, though, the same light that always gave Mella hope.

Mella and Sam walked back to the car where Paula waited. And as the buildings against the hillside became smaller behind them, an unspoken sadness filled the car. Paula felt it and chattered on about the school making Patty well, about the games the two would play together someday.

The house on Chatham Street really knew the void without Patty. When Mella suddenly found her workload easy, she put herself to work for neighbors, even becoming involved with Girl Scouts.

Early in the morning on Paula's fourth birthday Sam strolled into her bedroom, singing off-key, "Happy birthday to you!" He couldn't wait until after work to give her his present. Leading the sleepy girl to the kitchen table, he pointed to the box in the center, and without hesitating she ripped off the tissue paper and squealed at the roller skates inside.

Still in pajamas Paula hurried to the patio and tried out the new skates. Despite the many bruises and skinned knees, she was determined to become a champion of the patio set.

Now Mella had time to plan a real party. The neighbor children were invited—Kathy and Carol Murphy, Linda and Susie Johnson, and Donna's boys. After the cake and ice cream, all had sticky faces and hands to be washed in the wading pool.

When Sam would work late or serve on night duty, the wicker chair was moved again to the porch, and Mella would rock Paula. But no matter how lovely those times, the house felt empty without Patty. Mella moved to the porch in the evenings because it was hard for her to face the solitude inside.

How the family looked forward to their trips to Campo.

Juanita and Ted Gillam would accompany Mella when Sam couldn't go. Although they traveled the mountainous way through the National Forest, the heat still followed them.

The car's radiator would always boil over, so they chose those times for their picnic lunch. Once the motor cooled, away they would drive again toward the school.

While the women visited with Patty, Ted and Paula would play in the yard. He used to bribe her in his Missourian drawl, "If you're a good girl I'll show ya my sore toe." He never did, but it worked every time.

The journeys home were Paula's favorite, not only because of the cooling air, but as they traveled the narrow roads, her Uncle Ted would sing *Down in the Valley*. He had a round, merry face, especially when he puffed out his cheeks for the whistle on "Hear the wind blow." Paula never tired of the song, the whistle, or Ted's bribe about his sore toe.

Months passed, and in September on the way home from Campo, Mella commented that Patty didn't seem right somehow. She looked thinner, to be sure, and Mella was thinking seriously of taking Patty home the next trip.

Before that time came, however, she received a phone call from one of the attendants at the school. "The District Attorney is coming tomorrow to close down this place, Mrs. Bailey. You'll have to come and get your daughter. I'm sorry, but we tried. We just didn't have the help or the funds to keep the school going properly. Again, I'm sorry," she repeated.

Mella was stunned, yet relieved. Patty would be coming home! Then her hopes were dashed as she thought of the last visit. No progress had been made. Her daughter was still the same invalid.

When she and Sam stood at Patty's crib her odor sickened them. Mella quickly grabbed a fresh diaper, then gasped at the bedsores. Patty whimpered in pain, her round eyes full of an imploring look.

Mella couldn't help but cry as she followed her husband down the path to the car. Patty was soon put in the care of Dr. Meyers in El Cajon Valley. He began treating her for malnutrition, among other ailments.

When Jo Murphy crept to her kitchen window and parted the curtain, she sighed. "Poor Mella. It's when Sam's gone that Patty invariably acts up."

The lights across the gully guided her like a beacon as Jo made her way along the street. At the Bailey's back door she could hear Mella reciting, "Yea, though I walk through the valley of the shadow of death . . ."

Patty had been plagued by frequent spasms since coming home, and sometimes entire nights passed in which Mella never slept. But a surprise waited to warm this night.

"Jo! What are you doing up so late?"

As always, Jo Murphy sounded nonchalant. "Couldn't sleep anyway. Thought I'd keep you company awhile."

Mella smiled. "Thanks."

Soon another knock sounded at the door. It was Darlene Johnson. "Anyone for leftovers?" she asked.

"We never have leftovers at our house," Jo quipped. So, over a half-eaten casserole, the women shared their hopes and anecdotes about their children—all the ramblings that go with the midnight hour.

Mella watched from the sofa while Jo and Darlene took turns wheeling Patty around in her dilapidated buggy, soothing her and giving Mella a much needed rest for her long vigil ahead.

How could she ever repay these kind souls for their trouble? Of course, they would never accept payment—not these women. They were an independent sort, not really lavish in sympathy, but beneath all their talk Mella sensed an inaudible, "We care!"

# 10

Hurry, Paula, or we'll miss the boat!"

"I'm trying, Mommy," the girl puffed, picking herself up a second time from the gravel roadside.

Carrying Patty didn't slow Mella's pace any as she sped toward Coronado's ferry landing, Paula's short legs doing double time at her heels.

Under Dr. Meyers' care, Patty had regained weight and a healthy rose color to her cheeks. But that particular afternoon Patty's eyes looked listless after a siege of convulsions at the chiropractor's office on Coronado Island.

With Campo behind her, Mella had continued her quest for a cure, yet so far every hope was like a mirage leading her on without mercy. Now her hope rested in this practitioner whose treatments had been successful with certain brain-damaged children.

Since Mella's budget was limited she had to scheme and plot every move. She saved by parking in San Diego, riding the ferry as a pedestrian, then trudging to the chiropractor's office. Four quarters in the meter had always been sufficient—until this particular day.

With Patty's first convulsion, Mella feared the afternoon would be a washout. From then on conditions spiraled. Mella's tension mounted and Patty's convulsions delayed treatment, until finally the doctor gave up.

"I'm sorry, Mrs. Bailey, but I can't do a thing with her

today. Let's try again next week, OK?"

By that time Mella was certain her last precious minutes were ticking away on the parking meter. "Oh, I hope we can make it back before the police spot the car. All I have is one dollar left 'til payday."

Just as the boatman was casting off, Mella hollered, "Wait!" She scurried on board with the children, making her way to the stairs. There she stopped, gasping for breath, resting a few moments before ascending to the passenger deck.

As the ferry backed away from Coronado's greenery, the motor's purr, the bay, sky, and sea gulls all enveloped Paula like a grand balm. But not her mother. Mella's nerves were in knots. She saw nothing except the parking meter and the dollar left in her purse. *One scrawny dollar to buy bread and gasoline.*

They filed down the stairs early, and as soon as the ferry rocked to a halt, Mella and the girls were off, heading for the pier.

Had they made it in time? The answer lay under the windshield wiper in a neat envelope: PARKING VIOLATION—$1.00 FINE.

Angry tears burned Mella's eyes. "It wasn't my fault." Then she turned her gaze across the street to the sizable Spanish architecture that housed the police station.

"Come on, Paula."

The girl wanted to say, "Again?" but knew better.

In little time they were parading up to a teller's window.

"May I help you?" the lady asked politely, noting the child Mella carried and the other tugging at her hemline. With that Mella spilled out her story, doing her best to keep back the tears.

After she finished, the teller said, "Well, Ma'am, if you like, you could take your case to court. Perhaps the judge—"

"Forget it!" Mella retorted. She reached into her purse, pulled out the lone dollar and practically threw it at the woman.

Out they marched, Paula's eyes wide with astonishment.

She had never seen her mother behave like that.

Mella had settled into her spot behind the steering wheel when an envelope on the dashboard caught her eye.

"Not another ticket!"

When she opened it a five-dollar bill spilled out with a note:

> To help pay some of the transportation to bring your little girl to Coronado. I know that with God's help she will soon be well.
>
> A Friend

Suddenly, great remorse and relief came upon her, and tears flowed anew.

"Mommy, what's the matter?"

"The note . . . I'm so ashamed . . . and happy!"

That was beyond Paula's comprehension, her mother, claiming to be happy yet soaking the upholstery with tears.

Eventually, Mella was herself again. That frantic afternoon had been mended by one kind, short note, the writer forever remaining anonymous, but surely a perceptive and thoughtful person.

After several more chiropractic treatments, the therapist admitted that they weren't helping Patty and suggested a naturopathic specialist he knew.

Wandering into this new realm of natural remedies, Mella became educated in the properties of herbs, yogurt, and other health foods.

"The child hasn't been fed properly. Perhaps now, if she gets the right nourishment, nature will undo the damage and return her to normal," the man speculated.

Recalling her father's faith in herbs, Mella invested in the food that Patty promptly refused to eat. Even Cynthia Prince had little success feeding her. After weeks of mealtime frustration, Mella realized there was no change and dropped the treatment.

Then came a letter from Detroit that sent the Bailey household into a dither. Nonna was coming! So, in late November spring housecleaning began. Closets were tidied, beds aired, walls scrubbed, and floors waxed slick.

After working doggedly all week, Mella dressed the girls to match her spotless house, then headed for the train depot.

Soon they stood on a platform, Mella holding Patty while Paula, who was lost in a sea of suitcases and legs, clung to her.

"There she is!" Mella spotted the woman first. Nonna's sturdy shoes were clopping down the iron steps of the coach, landing a few feet from them.

"Meline! Meline!" she squealed and hugged them several times.

Settled in the car, Nonna filled it with a deluge of words. Mella slipped in an "Oh?" from time to time.

*So this is my grandmother,* Paula thought. She had already surveyed Nonna's attire, wondering about the coat and at least two sweaters she spied underneath. Now she was occupied with the flower atop Nonna's hat, bobbing with her every gesture.

When their car stopped in the driveway, Nonna shot out, "Oooo! Dis is a nicea house. Sam's doin' good in da Navy now?"

Then she spotted a neighbor coming across the lawn and beat a retreat back to the car. "Here, Meline! Quick! Let me take Patty inside before—"

Mella's cheeks flamed for an instant as she hugged her child tightly. Nonna's anxious face, combined with the nagging scene out of their past, caused Mella to retaliate more harshly than she meant to.

"Oh, no ya don't, Ma! Not here! This is *my* house. If people won't accept Patty, then they can just stay out."

Silence set in while Nonna brooded. *Why can'ta Meline understand? I always do des tings for her own good. I don'ta want her humiliated, that's all.*

A time of awkward adjustment followed for the grandmother. But she soon became accustomed to neighbors coming and going, of their gentle ways with Patty who usually greeted them all from the couch in the living room.

Around the middle of December Noonoon called to say he was ready for his son-in-law to fetch him. By that time

Sam had convinced his wife that Paula should go along with him to Michigan.

The cross-country trip created memories for the girl: Nonna and Mom kissing them goodbye; the back seat bed just for her; the steel bridge rushing past as they crossed high above the Big Muddy.

Then there was an incident that would become a well-worn tale over the years. Travel-weary Sam had rented a motel room. Wanting to get an early start, he rose at 4:30 a. m. and packed everything into the car, including Paula.

Somehow Paula slipped out of the car and stole past him, making her sleepy way again to the comfortable motel bed. Later, about 50 miles down the highway, Sam called, "Hey, princess. Time to rise and shine!"

No answer.

"Come on, lazy bones!" He reached back for an arm that wasn't there.

Without hesitating, Sam did a U-turn and sped back to the motel. Every fear imaginable tormented him. Had someone kidnapped his daughter while he was inside the motel? Had she wandered off somewhere and gotten lost? How would he ever tell Mella, who had objected to Paula traveling with him in the first place? His foot bore down on the accelerator.

Waking the manager, Sam got into the room. Relief flooded him when he spied Paula snoozing, burrowed deep under the covers and unaware of the anxiety she had caused her father.

Since the crisp air hinted of a fast approaching winter, the Baileys didn't stay long at Lake Higgins; only a day to help Noonoon close up the cabin. Then the three headed back to the West Coast.

When they arrived home Paula heard her mother's low voice as she buried her face in Sam's shoulder, followed by an, "Oh, Pa!" Then, although half-conscious, Paula could see her house in soft shadows.

"We're home—safe!" she mused.

Noonoon became a part of the Bailey household. How

Paula loved him—his gray, wiglike hair, his swooping mustache, the mothball aura that followed him, even out to the back patio where she delighted in his tales.

Gathering neighbor children occasionally for the story-fests, Paula would climb up beside her grandfather and plead, "Tell us about your first boat trip from Italy, Noonoon, when you were young."

A faraway look would fill his eyes, his tone reminiscent of the past he took pride in as he began, "Wella, it was lika dis . . ."

Every one of the children came alive and listened intently, never caring that the old man repeated himself, finding a comfort when the zany adventures led to Noonoon landing in "da great free country of America."

Patty, too, loved her grandfather. In fact, he worked the same special charm on her as Cynthia did, soothing her when needed and stirring her up at other times.

During the day Noonoon whittled and out of ordinary scrap lumber emerged fancy little men with mobile limbs, colorfully painted. The Bailey yard became the scene of windmills with the miniature fellows seesawing. The old man also crafted bird houses, and he and Paula enjoyed seeing the little warblers investigate their new homes.

One chilly evening, while they spied on a pair of sparrows, Noonoon remarked, "Come spring, dar willa be new bambinos in dat nest." Then he paused, a sudden twinkle lighting his eyes. "Dar willa be a new bambino in dis nest too, Paula."

She gave him a puzzled look.

He nodded, adding, "Anda Juanita too!"

The baby brother Paula had been praying for was arriving in May—and a new "cousin"! Now their family would be complete.

# 11

Never before had such a holiday dinner seen the Bailey kitchen on Chatham Street. The big Tom's aroma from the oven blended with familiar scents of tortellinis and home-made rolls, while salads, sauces, and pies added their tang from every available countertop.

Four young sailors, feigning patience, waited with the menfolk in the living room amidst dissected newspapers.

Only Ted Gillam wasn't there. He had crept back to the bedroom where Patty was being sheltered from the excitement.

"Ah, ha! So Miss Patricia just had her dinner in bed—like a princess. What a lucky girl you are!"

Patty beamed at the man.

"And now, I suppose you'll be taking a nap like a good girl should. In fact, if you go to sleep, Uncle Ted will show you his sore toe when you wake up."

"Aaaah!" Patty responded. She had been promised that before.

The giant fellow reached down and smoothed her hair. He wanted her to feel included in the festivities, but not enough to encourage a convulsion.

Ted's voice softened with sympathy, "Maybe someday, little girl, maybe someday . . ."

In the kitchen Nonna's apron fluttered before her ample form as she scuttled between the sink and stove, her high, shrill voice giving orders that few of the women took seriously. They were busy too, arranging dishes and mixing salads.

Their usual table was moved aside and replaced by a plywood board atop sawhorses. It was far from elegant, but a bleached sheet covering gave it a fine, clean look.

Paula's latest adopted aunt, Vada, busily cleaned Patty's tray. She was the helping hand who had spared Mella the task of feeding her daughter that noon. Either the oven's heat or her glowing spirit colored Vada's cheeks. She fully appreciated this new family she had wandered upon. A Swedish, round-faced woman with mischievous blue eyes, Vada possessed a competence that took over without asking. Rather brazenly, in fact, she just barged in, and Mella loved her for it.

When time came for them all to gather, silence fell upon the group while Sam said the blessing. It was his usual, but the feast of food and friendship gave the worn phrases a solemn sound.

Mella gazed around at the hungry faces, most familiar, some strange—like the sailors who hadn't been fortunate enough to get leave. At least their stomachs would find comfort that day at her overburdened table.

It was certainly an assorted gathering—Ted, Juanita, Vada with several of her friends, Mella, Sam, Paula, the sailors, Nonna like a jack-in-the-box, half eating, half serving, and, of course, Noonoon, his complacent, slow-paced self unchanged.

Despite its typical helter-skelter nature, this was Mella's home, these were her loved ones, and something warm filled her heart until she thought it would burst.

When the holidays faded, the Bailey household settled back into its semiroutine—except for Sundays. Preparing for church never worked smoothly. Even when Vada stayed over Saturday night to help with the next morning's activity, they were always late for Mass.

Like a ritual, the breathless threesome would rush in the door of St. Mary's, peer at the crowded pews, then climb the narrow steps to the balcony. That was fine with young Paula. She loved it up there, gazing down on all the heads. Time passed quickly in her imaginary eagle's nest where she would first count the white hats, next the dark ones, then the veils, and finally all the bald heads.

Mella would devoutly follow the proceedings in her prayer book, while Nonna, in her best jersey, well shrouded by sweaters and a coat, would sink into her own private world of prayer. She seemed totally oblivious to the priest, choir, and congregation alike.

Once in a long while Noonoon accompanied them, but usually he stayed home in his favorite niche on the back patio.

With the zeal of an evangelist, Paula confronted her grandfather one Sunday as he daydreamed in the morning air. "Noonoon, you should come to church with us, ya know."

A slow smile spread across the old man's face as he pulled the girl down to the swing beside him.

"Paula, you see dat little hummin' bird upa dar?"

She followed his gaze to the tiny bird dipping into blossoms on the trumpet vine, and nodded.

"Wella, do you know dose wings go back an' forta hundred times lika dat?" He snapped his fingers.

"Really?"

"You know, mi Pauline, I canna sit here and tink two hours 'bout dat birda an' 'bout da God Who maka dat birda, an' my heart, it lovesa Him more. Now don'ta ya tink dat's lotsa better dan bein' in an ol' churcha with lotsa peoples?"

Paula looked seriously into his lined face. "I don't know, Noonoon. We're supposed to go to Mass every Sunday . . . What ya said sounds good, though." Something about the miracle of the hummingbird touched her but she still wondered about her grandfather's odd religion.

Sam's lazy weekends soon ended after a certain middle-aged gentlemen visited. He was Pastor LeCompte, an ex-chaplain and newcomer to the community.

Sam warmed to him instantly. Here was a fellow navy

man, a comrade in the midst of civilians. Besides, Sam was impressed with the genuineness that flowed through the visitor's hearty handshake. "You can usually read a man by his handshake," Sam would say. And he was certain no false sanctity made up this minister.

After lengthy reminiscing about war days, Pastor LeCompte changed the topic. "Sam, I'm starting a Presbyterian church here in Fletcher Hills and I need your help. Are you with me?"

"Sure thing!"

Mella's eyebrows shot up in surprise. Was this her unorthodox husband speaking? He had hardly darkened a church door since their wedding. What had come over him? Well, it was all for the better, she supposed. They would have to pick an earlier Mass, because Protestant services started around 10:00. Or maybe Vada could come more often on weekends since she was considered part of their family now.

Sam's life soon turned to church activities, and eventually there were enough members to begin a building program. Land purchased atop a hill overlooking the community offered a perfect setting for their sanctuary, and Sam felt the exhilaration that accompanies such worthwhile projects.

One afternoon while Mella was helping her mother pluck the latest hens, Pastor LeCompte dropped by. After a brief greeting the man headed straight to the couch where Patty lay, took the girl's hand lovingly in his, and sat, looking thoughtful.

"Uh—may I get you something, Pastor?" Mella asked.

"No, thank you."

Feeling quite awkward about the situation, Mella stammered, "Is—is there something you wanted to see us about?"

"Well, sort of, Mrs. Bailey." The minister smiled at her. "Would you mind if I just sit here with Patty for a while and simply meditate?"

"I guess not." Mella looked puzzled while she shooed Paula outside to leave the minister and Patty alone in the living room.

Mella continued with her chores, still feeling uneasy

about the pastor's visit. Sam wouldn't be home for two hours to make some sense of this. Two whole hours!

Soon Noonoon arose from his nap and shuffled into the kitchen. "Whatsa Sam's priest doin' in dar with Patty?" he wanted to know.

"Shush, Pa! He's meditating."

"What's medadatin'?"

"I suppose he's thinking about God, Pa," Mella sighed with exasperation. "But I don't understand why he's doing it here."

Insight flashed into the old eyes. "Ah! I know. A good man, dat priest. A good man." Noonoon grinned broadly as he exited through the garage, so he wouldn't disturb the minister in the other room.

That afternoon marked the beginning of those unusual visits. Every now and then the pastor would show up and sit silently with Patty.

Once, as the minister prepared to leave, he intimated to Mella, "You just don't realize how much strength I receive when I come here, Mrs. Bailey."

"No, sir, I honestly don't."

Then he explained, "You see, Patty represents one of the innocent victims in the overall battle between good and evil, between Christ and Satan, if you will. Of course, so do all the other sick ones I visit. But Patty's so undemanding. And there's a certain serenity about her that helps me in thinking about holy things, about the blessings that God bestows upon us everyday." He cleared his throat before he continued. "It's a humbling of sorts. Actually, it's really hard to put into words, Mrs. Bailey, because I don't understand all the reasons myself. All I know is that it's easier for me to face the world every time I leave here."

The clergyman shook Mella's hand. "I thank you for these times with your daughter, Mrs. Bailey."

"You're welcome anytime, Pastor—anytime!" Mella's eyes sparkled with happy tears, her day sweetened by the dialogue.

After seeing him out, she gazed back at her daughter, now

asleep. "Saint Patty!" she whispered proudly.

As May warmed Noonoon's mornings on the patio, he began talking about Higgins Lake.

"Da snow is most gone now," he said several times a day, and Mella knew he wouldn't stay parted much longer from his beloved cabin in the woods. She dreaded the thought of his leaving, this man whose tranquil life calmed her own. And Nonna, who was always such a help, would have to go this time, leaving Mella to give birth without her mother nearby.

The fateful day arrived. The grandparents waved tearfully from their train window as Mella and Paula watched with sad hearts.

After the caboose disappeared, Mella scolded, "This isn't good. We mustn't mourn. We should be thankful for the months we've had with them. Your *zias* and *Zio* Carlo need to see their folks too, ya know. We mustn't be selfish with them. Come! Let's go to a restaurant!"

Paula's mouth flew open. *A real restaurant?* Such a treat was rare on their limited finances.

So the two drowned their sorrows in milk shakes and then drove home to a yard full of funny windmills and birdhouses and a kitchen stocked with spaghetti, all of which kept the memories of the wise Noonoon and industrious Nonna ever alive.

Sam had found a school near Chino that he said was ideal for Patty while Mella's time drew near. The expectant mother tired quite easily now, and although the previous experience of Campo still haunted them, Sam had convinced her about the school's merits, and she consented.

May seemed to be the month of partings, because soon Paula was kissing her sister goodbye and watching her vanish into a building nestled in tall woods.

Then came the day the girl was to stay with Mrs. Johnson while her mother went to the hospital "to get the baby."

No sooner had she drifted off to sleep when Sam's voice chimed, "Paula, you have a baby brother!"

Paula was delighted. "Oh, goody! Now we have our Little Sam."

During his wife's hospital stay, Big Sam was busy preparing a surprise for Mella. He had managed a deal on an entire bedroom suite—used, but in good condition. He looked like a little boy who had just picked a first bouquet for his mother when he set it up, fingering the vanity's blond wood, polishing its mirror, and smoothing the bedspread several times over.

Spying Paula's eager face, he warned, "Listen, young lady, this is a surprise for Mommy. Don't you dare tell her! Understand?"

"I won't, Daddy." And the girl reminded her father that she was nearly 5 years old, assuring him that she could keep a secret.

In front of the hospital Paula waited anxiously for her mom who was being wheeled out to the car, holding a tiny bundle in her arms.

In the car Mella turned back the receiving blanket so Paula could peek.

"Oh! You're pretty, Little Sam."

He was pretty for a boy: blond hair, blue eyes, a chubby round face, and his left cheek bore his father's dimple, as if the Great Sculptor had chiseled it there just for them.

Before the car turned onto the highway, the words escaped, "Wait 'til you see the surprise Daddy has for you, Mom! But I can't tell you it's a bedroom set, because . . ."

What had she done? Sam's face looked crestfallen as Mella scooted beside him to soothe him.

"Oh, Sam! Did you really? Is it true? I'm sorry it's spoiled, but I'll still act surprised—honest!"

"Yeah, but it just won't be the same," he muttered half-heartedly.

Soon the family was adjusting to the squalling at night, while Sam and Mella took turns with the feeding. When Paula heard the wicker rocker creaking during the wee hours, she knew her hungry brother was devouring another bottle of milk.

*Boy! He sure drinks a lot for a little kid!* she exclaimed to herself.

86

After about two months, when Sam junior no longer demanded the late feedings, his father decided it was time for Patty to come home, and decided to get her himself. He didn't return until the rest of his family was asleep.

When Paula awoke the next morning to the sight of her sister, lying in the bed next to hers, she cried, "Patty! Oh, Patty!" hugging and kissing her. Patty's arms flung about wildly in the excitement, and her voice made giggling sounds.

Soon their mother brought in Sam junior to meet his oldest sibling. Patty seemed to identify the little one. Her rosy cheeks swelled with smiles as she tried to focus on the baby.

The Bailey family had grown larger but, best of all, they were together again.

# 12

Take a look at her, Sam! She's worn to a frazzle."

"I know, Vada, but what can I do?" Sam felt uncomfortable, face-to-face with the ruffled woman.

"Yeah, Mella the martyr! Well, she's got to get help somehow. She can't go on like this. How about that place in Chino?"

"If you only knew how my wife suffers every time Patty goes away, you wouldn't even think—"

Vada snapped, "For Mella's sake, I would!" Then she saw it written all over his face, the awful fix he was caught in. *Poor Sam! Torn between a tender heart and practicality*, she thought.

Vada's tone softened. "I know the neighbors help, you help, I'm here on weekends. But that's not enough. There's just too much work involved with a baby and invalid under the same roof. Plus, there are all the other lives Mella can't help meddling in. Just look at that sewing she's volunteered to do!"

Vada gave an exasperated wave toward the pile of church bazaar materials waiting patiently in the corner.

Sam frowned. "Do you have any suggestions? I've tried, but you know how stubborn Mella is. And there's no way we can afford a private nurse." In that instant the answer came to him. "Mission Valley! It seems to me I heard something about a school there for handicapped children. Yep! Just on weekdays."

"Now you're talking, Sailor! That would be ideal. Patty could still be home on weekends."

And so it happened that Patty went off to school from Monday mornings to Friday afternoons. Paula's days were absorbed with the novelty of kindergarten, so it wasn't until their nightly prayer circle that she felt her sister's absence.

Paula began teaching Little Sam the hand motions to Patty's song, *Climb, Climb Up Sunshine Mountain*, but she missed taking hold of her sister's stiff arms and "climbing" with her. Sometimes on weekends they would sing Patty's song twice, and she responded with a double portion of her own sunshine.

Little Sam soon began to crawl about the house, pulling himself up at times, only to fall, cry with a brief passion, then plunge into life once more. His eyes grew larger and bluer by the day, the stout body firm and quite strong for his few months. Paula quickly learned to keep her distance when his temper flared.

There was one person, though, who could do most anything to Little Sam without repercussions. And that was Baby Virginia, the Gillams' new girl. She could strip him of his toys, pull his hair, and sit on him mercilessly, but Sam endured the torment like a gentleman, passively accepting it, surely thinking better days were ahead.

As the two toddlers romped in the playpen one day, Juanita felt a sudden inspiration. "Mella, what do you think about my doing Patty's hair?"

"Go ahead, Juanita. You've done it before."

"No, I mean, giving her a permanent."

Mella clapped her soapy hands. Permanents were quite the rage then, and it tickled her to think that her daughter could have an up-to-date hairstyle like other girls.

In no time pungent fumes penetrated the entire house while Juanita labored over Patty, finally propping her under a well-worn hair dryer.

When Paula came in from play that Friday afternoon, she found her exhausted sister soundly asleep under a head of fuzzy curls.

At 5:30 Mella glanced nervously at the clock. "Oh! I've got to hurry to the hospital to pick up Sam from work." She paused momentarily before asking, "Juanita, would you mind watching the baby and Paula? I think I'll take Patty along to surprise her father."

After a few hasty miles, Mella and Patty waited eagerly outside a ward. But two uniformed men, instead of one, headed toward the car.

"Mella, I'd like you to meet my doctor friend."

Introductions were made. Then Sam grinned at the curly head beside his wife. "Wow! Who's this good-looking gal here?"

Patty laughed up at her father.

"So this is Patty!" The commander studied the child as if lost in the sight of her. Had he known how that one glimpse would affect him, how it would leave an indelible image on his mind, he never would have been so eager to look her way.

Returning home, the doctor couldn't forget those eyes, those beautiful eyes that understood. He was certain they understood. It was more than a look of recognition she gave her father—much more. Sam had said she was completely palsied by age three. *Surely, she'd be severely retarded under those conditions*, he thought. But that spark of something undefinable needled him into the night until he resolved to explore Patty's case the next morning. He would pull her records, go over all past tests, then talk with his colleagues in neurosurgery. Perhaps there was hope yet for that lovely young daughter of Sam's.

At the Bailey home that evening, Patty became the main attraction. Word spread quickly, bringing friends to look at Patty's curls.

After all the attention, Mella wondered if she detected a look of vanity on Patty's sleepy face as she carted her daughter off to bed. Mella could hardly wait until Monday morning when she would take Patty to school. Her teachers would undoubtedly make a fuss over the hair-do as they did over anything new.

Mella was unaware of the sudden event in store that

would bring all her daydreams down to earth.

The next evening the Gillam family stayed for dinner, and all were contentedly chatting around empty plates afterward when Sam broke the spell.

"I have some news that could be good, but there's a bad part that goes with it," he began.

Mella looked curious. "Well, don't keep us in suspense, hon."

"Several of the doctors at the hospital think there could be a chance for Patty if they do a brain exploratory."

Mella gasped.

"Now, sweetheart, I've warned you before, and I don't know what good it will do now, but please don't go crossing any bridges ahead of time. Chances are pretty slim." Sam took a deep breath and continued. "The commander I introduced you to the other day was so taken with Patty that he started quite an investigation into her case, even made several phone calls back East to get all the details. Now he thinks a brain exploratory may just reveal the trouble. It's a long shot, but worth the try, I suppose."

Ted looked apprehensive. "What's the bad part, Sam?"

"First of all, Mella, I suppose you don't realize a brain exploratory means surgery, and anytime a general anesthetic is used there's a certain risk involved."

"Oh!" His wife's eyes widened, then met Juanita's. They were both thinking the same thing—Patty's new hair-do!

Mella was afraid to ask. "How much of her hair will they have to cut, Sam?"

"I'm sorry, but it'll all have to be shaved."

"Oh, no!" Both women groaned.

Quickly, Juanita put on an "I-don't-care" look, but she did care. All those pretty blonde curls would soon drop into an O.R. wastebasket. How dreadful!

But she assured Mella in her cheeriest drawl, "It'll be more than worth it if the operation helps Patty. After all, that's what we've been praying for. Hair grows back, ya know, and we'll just give it another wave when it does."

"You're right," Mella agreed, but quickly cleared the

table so she could flee to the other room and hide her tears.

After the Gillams left, Sam went out to the front porch where his wife sat, deep in thought. She hardly noticed the awesome silhouette the eucalyptus trees were etching against the setting sun.

"Mella, there's something else I need to explain before the surgery so you won't be shocked. The exploratory involves drilling six boreholes into Patty's skull, about the diameter of my little finger."

His words made Mella's stomach wretch. "Boreholes! Sam, that sounds hideous."

"I know. But it's what'll happen if we decide to go ahead with this thing."

"Oh, we'll have to go through with it, honey. If there's a chance in a million, we'd have to take it."

"OK, Mella. I figured you'd say that, so the operation is scheduled for Monday. We'll check Patty in quite early."

Together the couple watched the twilight in silence. Mella was pushing her thoughts aside. She had promised Sam that she would not fantasize this time. To the contrary, her visions weren't light, but dark and threatening as the words, "*certain risk involved*," returned again and again to trouble her.

But later in bed, when sheer exhaustion settled her fears, Mella let the daydreams have their way. *What if the operation is successful? What if we had a walking, talking Patty overnight?* Mella wondered at her own reaction to such a miracle when—*if* it should happen. Then she chided herself. She mustn't get charged with hope again. She mustn't!

The cross atop Mount Helix still gleamed in the darkness as Mella peered out the kitchen window and thought about the surgery that faced them that day.

Still, there was the same routine awaiting her. She fumbled with the breadbox, then popped two slices into the toaster. Patty could die today. Mella was wide awake now and acutely aware of the possibility. But what could she do? Then it came to her—the hospital chapel. She would seek out

92

the chapel and pray there during the surgery, but for now she just buttered toast.

The chapel seemed like a planet all its own, free from the antiseptic breath of the hospital. There Mella was alone with her God.

She bowed in prayer and fervently pleaded, "Please, Heavenly Father, help the doctors find the source of Patty's trouble this morning. Even if she could only talk, I'd be content, Lord. Please, make her well—please!"

For several hours her petitions soared heavenward. Then she remembered her husband had promised to meet her in a certain waiting room. Upon leaving she stopped at the door for a moment where some tracts caught her eye. She selected a few, thinking she might want to read them later on.

Mella's heart fluttered girlishly for a moment when she spotted Sam down the hall. Hastening toward him, she looked into his sober face, searching for his thoughts.

Why was Sam always so capable, so strong, when she seemed at the mercy of every emotion? It didn't really matter now. He was there and she felt safe.

Drawing her into the solarium, Sam told her, "Well, darling, before long the doctor should be here with a report."

Minutes passed like hours while Mella sat with hope and fear, waiting in the awful silence that pervaded the room, waiting for the sound of the surgeon's footsteps.

When he finally approached them, the couple stood together like two stone images, watching the doctor's face for any hint of the outcome.

"Sam, Mrs. Bailey, you don't know how sorry I am. We couldn't find one thing out of order, not one thing. I wish I hadn't even given you the hope."

Suddenly, it fell upon Mella, the shattering despair. She covered her face and wept. Her husband enfolded her and comforted without words.

"Oh, Sam, why doesn't God hear me?"

The doctor shifted his feet awkwardly. "I feel responsible. If only I hadn't interfered—"

"No! Don't say that!" Mella lifted her face. "It's not your

fault, and I'm glad we took the chance."

For the doctor's benefit she quickly repaired her tear-stained cheeks with a handkerchief. *The poor man must feel as bad as we do*, she thought.

"Mrs. Bailey," the surgeon's voice was gentle, "Patty will be out of Recovery soon. You may stay with her, if you like."

Soon Mella was sitting at her daughter's bedside, gazing at the still, gray head that was covered by a mound of bandages.

All at once she noticed something strange about Patty's breathing. She seemed to be gasping for air.

Mella fled into the corridor, crying, "Help! She's choking!"

A flurry of white uniforms rushed past her. Then she heard the doctor's voice, but it wasn't the same gentle one of before.

"What's the matter with you?" he blamed a nurse. "You know my orders were to lay her on her side."

Mella felt stunned as she watched from the background—the suction machine, oxygen tent, the white and khaki uniforms swirling before her. Finally, with his stethoscope again resting in place, the doctor assured her, "She'll be OK now, Mrs. Bailey. Don't worry."

"Thank you."

Again she was alone with Patty, who seemed to be resting comfortably under the tent. Remembering the tracts, Mella reached into her purse, deliberately stretching, trying to relieve the soreness in her back.

At first her tired mind couldn't quite comprehend the meaning of the messages she read, but then it dawned on her that these random choices all fit her present situation perfectly. "And we know that all things work together for good to them that love God, to them who are called according to his purpose" (Romans 8:28).

How many times had she read that verse in Sam's Bible, passing over it, not recognizing its wealth of meaning? Now the words brought new insight and strength.

She eagerly read on. "Nothing—no hurt, no joy, not even

death—can touch us unless God permits it. By allowing us to suffer at times, He smooths our rough places, molds us as a potter would, into a more perfect vessel. We become humble, patient, more tender and aware of our dependence upon Him."

Mella's thoughts rolled back over the years to the kind visitor at her parents' house in Detroit. The woman had defended God, said He wasn't a tyrant, that He wasn't the One responsible for all the hurt in the world. The visitor had used the word *allows*, also.

"But God permits," Mella repeated to herself, then focused on a tract about The Lord's Prayer. She had repeated Jesus' words, "Thy will be done," hundreds of times, but she hadn't meant them—not really.

Her uppermost conviction had been that Patty should get well. There was no other alternative, no possible good in the affliction. But now Mella viewed her child in a new light. Patty wasn't just a frail victim of cerebral palsy anymore, but an intricate, purposeful part in a great plan, so great that it was beyond Mella's mortal imagination.

Little by little the awful sorrow in her heart ebbed away until finally she slipped to her knees. "Oh, God," she whispered, "I've been so stubborn. Forgive me for it. Help me to accept Patty as she is, and please carry this cross with me, like your Word promises." Then she finished her prayer with a determined, "Thy will be done!"

Instantly, her own strong will fled, and nothing but a sweet look of resignation remained on her face. Her body was still tired, her back still ached, the operation had failed, and that hope was gone, but her horrible burden—all the years of searching, of blaming—was gone too. Now she felt free to love God as the great Father He truly was.

Mella returned home with a new air about her, one that even young Paula recognized. Later, when Patty's spasms came, Mella no longer tensed nor looked fearful. It was as if other Hands held hers and those of her daughter.

# CHAPTER
# 13

When chicken pox invaded their home that fall, the Baileys felt up to their brows in combat. Sam replenished the calamine lotion supply every evening and took over for his Florence Nightingale of a wife, who hovered relentlessly round the children's bedsides.

All three of the youngsters were affected at the same time, but the most miserable was Patty. Racked by the awful itching, she kicked and flung her arms almost continuously, crying for relief. Although Mella tried to keep the blisters moist with lotion, she couldn't be Patty's hands all the time, because her own health was failing from lack of sleep.

After about a week, the siege ended, and again their kitchen was filled with lighthearted chatter as if the whole unpleasant episode had been a nightmare, the only reminders being a few scars and an extra line or two in Mella's smile.

In October, Mac entered their lives. He was a beautiful specimen of a collie, and—much to his discredit—too good a guard. Apparently, in Mac's mind, he had mapped out his yard, and whoever set foot inside that boundary was dutifully branded with his sharp teeth.

It was hard to believe that someone as gentle as Mac could be anything but well-mannered. Even Patty thrilled to the touch of his ticklish fur and wet nose.

One day Mr. McElfresh, who had finished reading the electric meter next door, headed for the Bailey place. Heaving one leg over the fence, he spotted the collie making a beeline for him. There was nothing the poor man could do but stand aghast in that awkward position and watch the dog sink fierce teeth into his pantleg. What a surprise for Mac—and lucky for the man—that he had brought his wooden leg over the fence first! So ended Mac's brief stay on Chatham Street. Within hours he was discretely exiled to a ranch where his talents were more appreciated.

Never did the Baileys dream that Christmas of '51 would be their last together as a complete family. They were all there at tree-decorating time along with the enchanting glow that accompanies the task. Decorating took longer that year, mainly because of Little Sam's curious fingers that kept returning to pluck the tree's "forbidden fruit." Patty offered comments from her place on the couch, and when her father hung a last tinsel and connected the colored lights, Patty's eyes outsparkled the brightest of ornaments.

First thing Christmas morning, two boisterous children sprang up to discover their presents. Then their sleepy parents brought Patty in to join them. Little Sam and Paula took turns opening their sister's gifts while Patty responded with her usual "ah," but there was something of a lilt, something musical in her voice that morning. Mella wondered how much she simply responded to their festive mood and how much she really understood.

In the spring, there came a new turn in their lives. Sam received orders for Hawaii.

"Hawaii? Oh, no!" Mella complained.

Sam was puzzled. "I thought you'd be overjoyed." Then he grinned. "Nine years of marriage, and I still can't figure you out!"

Mella was thinking of Fletcher Hills, of all her beautiful friends. "I can't leave. I just—"

Her husband stopped the protest with a kiss. "Cheer up! We'll simply rent out this house for a couple of years. Chances are pretty good that we'll come back here."

It took a while for Mella to accept the idea of moving. Falling for a sailor did have its disadvantages, she thought, but then smiled at a long-forgotten reproof. Nonna had said, "Remember, Meline! You make a your own bed. Now you're gonna have ta lie in it—all over da world with dat man of yours!"

Of course she would always follow Sam, the incurable romantic that she was. But to her, Hawaii definitely was at earth's end, and leaving bosom friends, even temporarily, was going to be a sacrifice.

Young Paula wasn't sure about the significance of the trip, but after hearing Mrs. Murphy say something about paradise, she concluded Hawaii must be where Adam and Eve had lived once, so she spread the word to fellow first graders.

One of the first things the Baileys did was buy a car, a small blue Austin convertible, that could easily be transported with the family across the ocean. It was the first "new" car they had owned, and they all were quite proud of its unique place in the neighborhood.

Then came a sad day for them, when Donna and Earl had to leave. Mella blinked back tears when she hugged her friend. "You won't be that far away, Donna. Now, don't forget to call!"

"I won't, Mella. I just want you to know how much your family has meant to us—"

"Donna! Who's the one I caught washing my dishes so many times? So many times . . ." she repeated wistfully. "*I'll* never forget."

A long silence followed in which tearful smiles were exchanged and thoughts were allowed to wander back over their rich friendship. And when the last goodbye was said, those memories would hover around the house next door, keeping it Donna and Earl's place a long while.

Orders called for Sam to leave a month ahead of his family, and before that, he was to be stationed for a week near San Francisco.

One evening Sam remarked, "You know, Mella, even though we're almost broke again, I think we could manage that week in an Oakland motel."

"You mean—all of us?"

He reached out for Mella and drew her close. "Sure! It's gonna be a whole month, darling, before I get to have ya'all with me again. I'd have to spend the days on base, but at night we could see the sights of San Francisco. How's that sound?"

"Great, Sam! But a motel. That seems so expensive, so frivolous."

"Hush!" he ordered. "We can afford to be frivolous just this once."

And so they enjoyed their week together in San Francisco with its Golden Gate Bridge, vertical streets, and trolley cars.

By Friday morning their money had nearly run out. Mella regretted leaving Sam behind without a proper farewell from dock, but she hid her disappointment by saying, "If we go now, we'll miss the weekend traffic."

Amid many "I love yous" and tears, Mella and the three children piled into the Austin, oblivious to what waited a few miles down the road.

*Crunnnch!* It came at an intersection, hurling all of them backward. Mella regained the wheel and edged over to the curb just in time to catch a sharp profile of the offender as she passed her and headed out of sight.

"Why, of all the nerve!" Mella steamed. After checking the children for injuries, she got out to survey the damage done to the car.

Little Sam was blubbering while Patty looked on, seemingly amused by the fuss. Heavyhearted, Paula watched her mother wander around the automobile a few times. Finally, she returned in angry tears.

"Oh, Paula! I can't even go 10 miles without getting in an accident." Then she looked deep into the small, anxious face. "The trunk! It's all mashed in."

Just then they heard it, like a rare bird calling from the midst of Oakland's traffic, "Yoo hoo! I wanna see you!"

There sashayed a woman toward them, her features all smiles. "Hellooo!" she sang out. "I'm the one who bumped into your little ol' car."

"I know!" Mella bit her lip. She despised the blasé sound of the woman's voice. It only made the accident and the trip's delay seem worse.

The offender went on to explain that her insurance agent was located a few blocks away. He was waiting for them to discuss the claim.

Two boring hours later Mella fed her children the peanut butter sandwiches she had packed, then pulled out onto the road.

Dark came slowly to the Pacific sky as the small auto headed southward. They were nearing Ventura where Mella hoped to refuel. By then Sam junior and Patty slept peacefully in the back seat, leaving Mella and Paula tired comrades on the road.

Nervous tension from the accident had caught up with Mella; she felt drained but had the will to go on.

At the gasoline station, she checked her purse. "Let's see. I have just enough for gas again . . . How about some milk for your supper, Paula?"

The girl grinned in approval while watching a man clean their windshield.

"Uh, Ma'am," the attendant addressed Mella, but was eyeing the children anxiously, "were you planning to go much further tonight?"

"Down to San Diego," Mella replied.

"Well, a couple of convicts escaped near here and they're believed to be quite dangerous. Police are warning motorists not to stop along the highway or to pick up any hitchhikers."

"Thank you." That ruined Mella's plans of napping along the way. And since she had no money for a motel, she had to keep driving. Then she turned to Paula with a reassuring smile. "Well, let's go get that milk, young lady."

Afterward, their faithful Austin thrummed on. A full moon hung low over the Pacific, making a ragged path of silver through the sea, its dark waves reaching into nothingness. How small and insignificant Mella felt. Paula was just describing the silver path, how it was following them,

gabbing about anything to keep her mother awake when—
the girl fell asleep.

An awful drowsiness came over Mella. Suddenly a horn
blast brought her eyes back to the road, then to the rear-view
mirror where she spotted a semi towering over her small
Austin. For miles he followed her, flicking his lights, sounding his horn, keeping watch on the little vehicle like a giant
mechanical angel.

Finally, Mella spied a cafe and pulled off the road. The
truck roared past her, giving one final blast for goodbye. She
looked after him with eyes of gratitude. From then on, in her
mind, truck drivers were first-rate, ranking somewhere next
to priests.

Mella needed to walk around for a few moments, get her
blood circulating. Then it was back to the wheel, back to the
highway. Only a few more hours to go.

She sensed something ominous about the night, as though
it were a villain challenging her, "You'll never make it."

"Oh, yes, I will!" she called out, then looked anxiously
around at her sleeping flock. Down the coast she continued,
softly singing the peppiest tunes she knew, stopping only to
slap her numb cheeks and to offer an occasional prayer.

Finally, San Diego's familiar fog closed around her.
Funny, it should seem so comforting, this thick screen that on
other nights had been nothing but treacherous. Now it meant
Fletcher Hills was near. With a loving hand, Mella patted the
dashboard and thought how dependably the small car had
performed. And now, like a wounded soldier, it was winding
its way homeward after battle.

Finally, there was Highland Drive, the key, the porch
light, and her bed, where she dreamed about trucks, prison-
ers, and the moon dancing wildly above dark waves.

Mella had been too exhausted to notice that her new
neighbors had arrived. Getting acquainted the next day, she
excused her haggard appearance, explaining a little about her
night's journey.

Doris listened, then shyly asked to watch the Bailey

children while Mella rested. Doris' daughter, Linda, was nearly Paula's age.

"Thank you." Mella smiled. "But that's OK. I can manage." She was surprised by the offer. Evidently, Doris would fit nicely into their friendly neighborhood—no coaching necessary.

*Brring!* The telephone shattered the afternoon calm.

"Sam? You're kidding! OK!"

Mella couldn't believe what she had just heard. Her husband's ship hadn't left as scheduled, and he had obtained liberty for the weekend. Now he was in San Diego at the bus station.

Soon they were all scrambling for Sam's arms, while Mella sobbed out the whole story of their traveling ordeal the day before. When they pulled into the driveway, Sam wrapped his arms around Mella. "You know, sweetheart, you're really some great gal."

"But, Sam," Mella wailed, "our new car's ruined!"

"The insurance'll pay for it, and soon it'll be as good as new."

The rest of the weekend they relaxed around the house, except for spending a few moments with their new neighbors. Sam seemed to spend more time than usual with Patty, holding her, rocking her, tickling her.

Monday morning dawned serenely enough. At 8:35, Sam was shaving, preparing for his bus trip back to San Francisco.

"Honey!" he called from a face half-lathered. "Would you phone the bus station? Find out if the bus really does leave at 9:30."

Mella gasped and put down the receiver. "It leaves in fifteen minutes!"

"I was afraid that man gave me the wrong time on Friday." Sam scooped up his son in one arm and his duffel bag in the other. "Let's go!"

Patty, still in pajamas, was in the middle of breakfast. Mella stared momentarily at the face and top splattered with oatmeal, then hurried next door. Before she got half her frantic story out, Doris waved her on.

"I'll finish feeding Patty and watch her 'til you get back. Don't worry about anything!"

"I shouldn't be long," Mella called over her shoulder. "Thank you!"

So the little Austin headed west, this time with unusual speed. Just as the car rounded the corner to the station, a bus pulled out into traffic.

Mella groaned. "It's the one to Long Beach. We missed it."

Sam was his typically composed self. "Calm down. We'll chase it to La Jolla, and I'll catch it there."

The Austin strained to keep up with the Greyhound, but 50 miles per hour topped its usual cruising speed. All along the way—La Jolla, Oceanside, San Clemente—the Baileys lagged behind by a few crucial minutes.

Finally, pulling into the Long Beach station, they paraded in double-time to the ticket counter.

"Whew!" Sam sighed. "There's a whole six minutes 'til the bus leaves. I'll get in line."

It was then that his son announced, "I gotta go bad."

The anxiety on his small face prompted Mella to move the boy quickly to the Ladies' room. There she experienced one of the clumsiest episodes in her life. Suddenly, she was all thumbs. She, a professional seamstress, fumbling with endless buttons! What had ever possessed her to think button-down trousers were fashionable for little boys? She hated buttons—especially now.

Meanwhile, the driver cast an impatient look toward Sam, the only passenger left outside the bus. Still no sign of Mella from the restroom.

Finally, he gazed down at Paula sniffling next to his duffle bag and gathered her up, kissing a tear away. "You be a good girl," his voice choked. "Take care of your mommy. I love you. See ya in Hawaii, princess!"

She watched him disappear into the dark bus, and kept her hand in motion until her mother came running breathlessly to her side.

Mella groaned. "I missed kissing him goodbye!"

Taking that as a cue, Little Sam let out a wail that echoed throughout the station. There was no pacifying him, much to the disgust of passersby.

"That's OK, Mama," Paula said, "I kissed Daddy for you, and he told me he'd see us in Hawaii."

Mella looked for the nearest exit. She wanted out of there, away from gaping faces, where she and her son could mourn in private.

All at once it dawned upon her, "Patty!" She ran to a phone booth and called Doris long distance, explaining what had happened.

Mella headed back to the highway. Lately they seemed drawn to that road, ever struggling against it, always hurrying home.

Several times she voiced her worry. "Poor Doris! I hope she doesn't have any problems." *What if Patty had spasms? How would Doris cope with her?* Mella fretted the entire trip.

At last, around 5:00, they arrived in the driveway.

Doris appeared immediately. "Patty's over here," she called, then added, "I have supper ready for you."

When Mella walked into Doris' house, all she saw was the radiant face of her Patty, looking contented and clean.

Linda was peeking bashfully from behind her mother. "We had fun giving Patty a bath," she revealed. "Then we made all your beds and did your dishes, and—"

Mella collapsed onto the nearest chair. She had been so concerned, and here this near stranger had taken over just as one of her Fletcher Hills' family would have. Such kindness overwhelmed her, bringing a flood of tears. They were tears of gratitude, of relief, of just plain weariness.

Doris gave Mella a gentle squeeze that said, "I understand."

# CHAPTER
# 14

It's a good institution, Mella. In fact, I think it's the best place possible for Patty."

"Vada, do you know what you're asking me to do? I can't! I can't leave her behind, not my own daughter!" Mella nervously paced the kitchen floor, her tormented eyes looking anywhere but at her friend.

"Then tell me how you're going to manage a small son, an 8-year-old invalid, as well as your luggage on a train, and then on a ship's journey. Tell me!" In Vada's earnestness, in her love for Mella, her face was set with determination that was somehow tender despite her stern words.

"I'll—I'll get help along the way."

"Oh, Mella! Be reasonable! A porter or two wouldn't help much. And think of poor Patty, being lugged from one depot to another. Do you think that would be fair to her?"

Mella sat bitterly silent. She knew her friend's case was ironclad, but how could she bear the thought of an ocean between her and her precious child?

The Baileys had visited Pacific Colony before Sam's departure and were impressed with its green lawns and lovely Spanish-looking buildings. They both had commented on its many benefits, including the friendly staff and well-equipped hospital. But the prospect of Patty going there was left up in the air—until now. Vada, far more realistic than Mella, knew the pitfalls ahead if Patty were to travel. She wanted Mella to enjoy Hawaii, to make it a time of rest, of renewal.

For another hour the verbal tug-of-war continued, Vada using every possible persuasion until Mella gave in.

"All right! You win. I know it's what Sam thought best, but he couldn't stand my being hurt again." Then she sobbed, "Oh, my dear, dear Patty! I'll miss you so much."

Vada cried too, but she was relieved, knowing that Patty would be under excellent supervision and that Mella's trip would be carefree. Playing the part of prosecutor had been rough on Vada. Now she could relax and act as sympathizing friend again.

Time came too soon for the departure. Vada insisted upon driving, giving Mella every last moment with her daughter.

When Paula and Sam junior kissed their sister goodbye, she flashed her own sweet smile—then was gone. Doris understood Paula's need to be alone and enticed the other youngsters outside.

The 7-year-old sat for a long time in the center of her sister's deserted things, the mute pinafore hanging lonesomely in the closet, her doll that prayed, "And make me better everyday," the folded roll-away bed that had held Patty for years, now looking forlorn. Soon the movers would come and take them all away.

Everything was novel and exciting to the children, the thronging feet along deck, the eager chatter and farewells, the tugboats far below, pushing the ship out of port. And there were Mella's quiet tears for Patty and for the home she had left temporarily behind.

Down in the corridors they could feel distinct motion under them as they searched for their cabin. Another chief's wife waited for them there. She would share quarters with Mella and her two children, a place equipped with two bunk beds, lockers, their own bathroom, and a porthole that provided a dreamy view of clouds and sea.

The first evening was serene. On deck the Baileys watched the setting sun spread gold above the seascape.

But the next day turned wild. The waters whipped into a

frenzy, tossing the ship from side to side, as if it were a toy. Walking was risky and everyone became seasick, even sailors guarding the hallways. They sat miserably over buckets at their posts, looking as green as the passengers.

For days Mella and the two children barely ventured from their room. Finally she decided that fresh air was in order, so despite their weakened condition, they climbed the stairs to the deck.

Carrying Little Sam, Mella stepped out into the open air. Suddenly, the ship lurched and she tripped, sending her son flying toward the guardrail. An M.P.'s helmet bounced across deck as he dived for the boy.

"Oh! How can I ever thank you?" Mella's voice trembled.

The young sailor responded with hidden pride, "It's my job, ma'am. Don't mention it."

But she did—every time she went topside. There was a special rapport now between the Baileys and this sailor who had saved Little Sam.

One night what sounded like screams filled their cabin. Paula buried her head under the pillow and lay still for what seemed like hours. Suddenly, light glared overhead and Mella yelled, "Get it! Get it!"

What was happening? Curiosity forced Paula to peek down from her top berth at the chief's wife. She was trying to grab something—something small, something red—Little Sam's fire engine! Apparently, the toy had become dislodged and was freely traveling the floor with every roll of the ship. Finally, the chief's wife snatched up the vehicle, and after much giggling, everyone settled back to sleep.

Sometime during the last night of the voyage, the wind settled and the waves were calm. An entirely different world greeted them when they awoke. The motion was gone, the monotonous rolling of the vessel, and they could enjoy a peaceful breakfast in the dining hall.

Afterward the Baileys climbed above where other passengers gathered on deck to watch the island of Oahu grow out of the vast blue of ocean.

First it was a hueless hump, then green, then alive with tropical loveliness. Buildings took shape. Finally people were clearly outlined on the dock below. Paula was first to spot her father squinting up at the crowded rail.

It took forever to disembark. In fact, the Austin made it off before Mella and the children. Finally, they were all crumpling Sam's starched khakis, the four of them talking at once.

Then the Baileys made their way through Honolulu, over the Pali, and down through the flowered streets of Kailua. Their destination, Kaneohe Marine Corps Air Station, looked typically military with its Quonset huts and barrack-type buildings—except for Mokapu's crater jutting out of the sea at the base's edge.

Living out of suitcases and sleeping on borrowed mattresses, the family managed until the movers arrived. Then their new surroundings became cozy with the familiar couch, chairs, and kitchen table.

Their place quickly filled with friendly folks, and there was something reminiscent of Fletcher Hills in the housing project.

And each night a lone bugle would wail, sounding *Taps* through their bedroom windows. The notes seemed to linger long, caressing the village that slept between dark beaches. It was the mournful, nostalgic sound that sent their thoughts to Patty. *Was she happy? Did her attendants play with her and love her as her family did?*

Mella spoke of Patty often. One day a neighbor, Doris Bulletset, commented, "I have a sister who lives in Ontario, California, Mella. Her name's Joyce, and she just might be interested in visiting your daughter."

Mella brightened. "Do you really think she would? Just to know how Patty's doing would be such a comfort!"

"I'll write her today," Doris promised.

At best, all Mella expected was an occasional visit. But Joyce Samuelson proved to be of rare stock. Faithfully, every Sunday afternoon, Joyce traveled to Patty's bedside and visited the girl who was, at first, a stranger to her. Then she followed with a letter, reporting on the child's health, of any little incident that might encourage the Baileys.

> *Patty is really fond of the music box you sent. I told her Anchor's Aweigh was her father's song because he's a Navy man, and she smiled. There's a girl named Gilda who's particularly attached to Patty, and I'm sure the feeling is mutual.*
>
> *Gilda is one of the patients herself, and spends long hours with your daughter, making sure she's comfortable, talking and singing to her. So, you see, Patty's getting lots of love and attention.*

Mella wondered about this person, Joyce. What a saint she must be! She intended to meet Joyce someday and try to express the comfort her letters brought.

Except for the proverbial roaches in the shower and ever-constant mosquitoes, Hawaii lived up to its reputation. Paula went barefoot to school, enjoying tropical sunshine and breezes. Oftentimes they ate supper at Kailua Beach and romped for hours at the water's edge, their only care being the destruction of a sand castle.

Always uppermost in Mella's mind was the weekly letter from California.

> *Dear Mella, Sam, and children,*
> *Patty just passed through another bout with pneumonia. Doctor said it wasn't serious this time—a light case.*
>
> *She's back to her old self. When she smiles, the whole room lights up. Her big, brown eyes twinkle like stars again. So I know she's OK.*
>
> *Please stop thanking me. You know these visits give me the satisfaction of not wasting my time, of doing something worthwhile. I can't help but love Patty. In fact, all the nurses and aids at the colony feel the same as I. She might not communicate like us, but words aren't always necessary to convey feeling.*
>
> *Tell my sister, Doris, we all send our love and miss her and family.*
>
> *Joyce*

Unexpectedly, the Korean War broke out and soured the good times. Sam was sent off on a battleship to the war zone for six months' duty. Meanwhile, air raid drills interrupted Paula's school days, with treks to a bomb shelter carved in the side of a mountain. It was all exhilarating to the children, who didn't understand the peril across the waters.

No sooner had Sam left than Mella's right arm began to ache. After days of misery, she finally went to a doctor.

"It's bursitis, Mrs. Bailey, and X-rays show a bone spur on your elbow, compounding the situation." He then went on to explain treatment, which consisted of pain pills and rest.

The drug caused a grogginess that Mella despised. Anything that curbed her inbred vivaciousness she considered evil, so she held off taking the medicine until the pain became unbearable.

One day, after an especially good letter from Joyce, a telegram came that shocked them. Patty was sick again, dangerously so, with pneumonia. She wasn't expected to live.

At once the miles to the states became endless. Mella felt helplessly alone. Why did Sam have to be out to sea now when she needed him so desperately? There was no one to turn to except the chaplain.

Father Reed, usually a rascal of a priest, easy-going and quick-witted, offered Mella the counsel she needed, showing a special tenderness and sympathy.

"Mrs. Bailey, God is just as close to your little one in Pomona as He is to us right now. And Jesus can heal that arm of yours, too, if we only ask Him. Let's pray!"

Mella found it hard to concentrate on Father Reed's words, but she left the chapel that day lightened of her burden. Amazingly, her arm quickly began to mend. Mella's only thoughts then were for Sam. *Had the Red Cross notified him yet? Would he be able to come home if—*No! She wouldn't think that. She must have faith.

# 15

When the grim face of the executive officer met Sam's, he knew something was terribly wrong.

"Bailey, I've a message for you. It's not good news, sir." He handed a dog-eared note to the corpsman. *Chief of Naval personnel says your daughter in Pomona is critically ill. It's pneumonia.*

For a moment panic seized Sam. *Patty! She was dying—a half-world away.*

The executive officer continued, "Everything's arranged. The Captain has the go-ahead for a copter to pick you up from ship and fly you to a carrier. From there, it's to Japan and then on to L.A."

Sam felt stunned. His daughter, her bright face, the helicopter, carrier, jets, the shock set all these images awhirl. He couldn't seem to get a grip on his thoughts.

"Uh—I'd like to have some time to think about this, sir. Then I'll let ya know."

The officer looked puzzled. *Time?* He would have jumped at the chance to fly stateside, especially if his child's life were on the line. Well, the news was sudden. He guessed he could understand the chief's hesitancy.

"OK, Bailey. Only don't take too long. The chain of command is waiting for the go-ahead, you know."

Then the officer was gone, leaving Sam alone in his quarters, alone with the cold, ugly facts. Patty was dying. His own dear Patty. He longed to hold her at that moment and hope for one last flicker of recognition from those eyes that had always radiated nothing but love for him.

Ambling over to the porthole, Sam stood brooding out at the elements. It was the rainy season. For days a downpour had kept the sea churning, with no letup in sight. In this torrent at least three pilots, perhaps a chopper crew, would brave flights for his sake. How could he gamble so, put those lives in jeopardy for one selfish glimpse of his daughter alive? And would she still be alive by the time he reached Pomona?

A sardonic smile twisted at his lips. He was recalling another time aboard ship, eight years before, when he would have given a month's pay for the opportunity he had now—just to see his baby girl. He wouldn't have considered the dangers then. Through flood and fire he would have strove like a Spartan just to hold her for a few moments.

What had happened to him? Had he grown callous over the years? No. He loved his Patty more than ever. His whole being ached for her, ached for the chance to see her smile to his "How's my gal?" one last time. But could he put those pilots and crew in danger simply to take him to the bedside of his daughter? The thought of their bravery warmed him, and new hurt swelled in his throat as he considered *their* families.

Drawing the cabin door shut, Sam knew he had to pray, he had to give this monster of a problem over to God. After all, he had learned as a boy, *God is our refuge and strength, a very present help in trouble.* He couldn't remember the exact psalm, but that didn't matter just then. Only the Lord knew the end from the beginning, if Patty's time was over. So he knelt down by his bunk and buried his face in his hands.

His prayer was simple, "Father God, I don't know what to do. So many people would risk their lives for me. Please, tell me!"

No sooner had he uttered the words than a warm peace enveloped him. He was certain he had the answer. Grabbing his hat, he rushed out and made his way to the quarters of the executive officer.

"Sir," came the breathless address, "thank you for everything, but Patty's had pneumonia before. I know she'll make it."

The officer grunted, on his face obvious disbelief. "Bailey, the Red Cross said it was urgent. They know—"

"Excuse me, sir, but the risk involved for everyone is too great. There's no way I could be a party to it. Anyway, I'm sure my daughter will come through OK." Then he added with a smile of gratitude, "I thank you so much for all the trouble you've taken to arrange things. I really do appreciate it, sir."

The executive officer frowned and shook his head, "OK, Bailey. If that's the way you want it. I'll pass along the word." *A strange one, that chief! He certainly didn't look like a distressed father. In fact, he looked rather pleased, as if he had some inside information. Well, moments of stress do funny things to people,* the officer concluded to himself.

Sam realized this man, as well as the rest of the sailors, would think him cold and uncaring, but he had an assurance from a Higher Source than they.

For 47 hours Sam waited, each hour passing at a snail's pace. When doubts sprang up he refused to give way to them.

Finally, the radiogram came: *Patricia passed crisis. Out of danger.* Those few words were all Sam needed to keep him going until he could see his daughter again.

Mella, too, received the news. She could hear the happiness in Joyce's voice over the phone, despite her sounding as if she were calling through a long tunnel. "Mella! It was close this time, but she made it!"

"Thank God!" the mother cried. Although their conversation was brief because of the expense, Mella managed to convey her appreciation to Joyce for her visits and letters.

"As I've written, Patty does more for me than I do for her. She's a blessing to know," Joyce responded with emotion.

When Mella put down the phone, she felt touched by the concern of a woman who had, only a few months before, been a stranger. And the irony was that Mella had never laid eyes on Joyce. She had no idea what her friend looked like, but she had seen her spirit, time and time again—a caring, beautiful spirit.

Patty had made it. Their prayers were answered. They had been given back the privilege of seeing their loved one again as soon as the Hawaiian tour was over.

Sam returned unscathed from the war zone, and the Baileys spent much of the remaining time sightseeing. He had invested in a movie camera and was fast turning family and neighbors into stars with the enchanting island of Oahu as a backdrop.

One day the marines put on an exhibition for base dependents. Mrs. Reddinger, with her twin girls, sat with Mella and her children. She had a hectic time keeping her lively twosome from joining the marchers.

They especially enjoyed the troops' valiant and muddy efforts through an obstacle course. Also, their band music was invigorating, but didn't exactly fit the tropical setting.

To make the day complete, a letter from Joyce awaited their return home. Mella's eager voice read aloud.

*"For a while Patty didn't respond much, so I knew she didn't feel back up to par. But this last Sunday she was all smiles—especially when I sang,* Climb, Climb Up Sunshine Mountain *to her."*

When Mella finished the letter, she exclaimed, "Well, our girl is back to normal. It won't be long, children, before we'll see her again."

Time passed quickly. In a few days a surprise bon voyage party was given for Mella. Then the moving van came to empty the house of everything but the bare necessities.

When the Baileys drove through the gate of the air station for the last time, Mella turned to her daughter and said, "Don't look so sad, Paula. We may meet our friends again on the mainland sometime. Anyway, think about Linda and Susie Johnson and the Murphy girls you'll be seeing soon."

Paula couldn't muster even a feeble smile. All the days of swimming and picnics by the beach were fast fading into a happy past that she guessed would never be repeated during her childhood. And the prospect of returning to Fletcher Hills seemed too remote at that moment.

Temporary housing at Baker's Field helped them appreciate the home they had at Kaneohe. The roaches here made the others look like midgets. Mosquitoes, too, took on dive-bomber proportions as they stung repeatedly at night.

During the day, Sam junior and Paula played on nearby gym equipment. When a deaf boy joined them one afternoon, the children had fun communicating with their own innovative sign language.

The deaf child's mother and Mella sat together and were soon wrapped in conversation.

"Your children are amazing," she told Mella. "I've never seen kids try to talk with Bobby that way. Usually, they just avoid him."

Mella welcomed the chance to tell the woman about Patty, explaining that such a sister had probably made her children tolerant and, perhaps, more tender toward the handicapped. Then she asked, "How about Bobby? Has he been receiving special education?"

"Well, no," the mother confessed. "I keep him at home. His father and I manage him pretty well."

Although Mella was fully sympathetic, inside she was bursting with advice. She wondered if she should mind her own business, then decided not to.

"You know, by sheltering your child, you're stunting his growth." Mella, ignoring the woman's surprised expression went on. "Believe me. I know what you're going through. I've been there. You feel protective, that you're the only one who can care for Bobby, the only one who can teach him and really love him. But it's not so. You're fortunate that his handicap is small compared to my Patty's. With the proper training, Bobby can lead a near normal life. But you have to be willing to let go a bit, give him room to learn from capable teachers."

On and on they talked until it came time to leave. Bobby's mother left them with, "Thank you, Mrs. Bailey. You've opened my eyes today. My husband will be grateful. He's been after me since Bobby turned seven, but I was so afraid the world would hurt him."

"I know," Mella replied, her eyes misty.

The band was warming up when the Baileys arrived at the dock to wait their climb aboard the U.S.S. *Ainsworth*. The crowd milled around them, people draping leis on one another, then embracing. Paula gazed up at her father, who looked handsome in his uniform. He was going with them this time, not in the same cabin, but on the same ship.

Through all the strangers emerged a familiar sight, Mrs. Reddinger with her two daughters. "Oh, Mella!" she gasped. "I was afraid I wouldn't make it in time." Then she put leis over their heads, leis that she had made herself, their ginger scent adding a certain nostalgia to the moment. After hugging her and the twins, the Baileys climbed the gangplank.

"Remember, Paula," Mrs. Reddinger called, "if your lei touches shore, you'll come back."

The superstition pricked the young heart. Paula was eager to return to Fletcher Hills, but why did she have to leave all this behind?

She wasn't the only one shedding tears as the ship pulled away from the dock, and notes of *Anchors Aweigh* floated up to the passengers bidding farewell. Off came Paula's lei to join the others in the water. Fervently, she wished for hers to touch shore. Further and further away the ship glided until the leis blurred and the last notes of *Aloha Oi* drifted out over the harbor.

# CHAPTER
# 16

San Francisco before dawn seemed like a fairyland, with hardly a sound coming from the sleeping buildings that huddled together along steep hillsides. The Golden Gate Bridge also looked unreal, like some huge mural. Only the cool mist made Mella's dreamy senses come alive.

When the city awakened hours later, the Bailey family disembarked, anxious to get down the coast to their Patty, and then on to Fletcher Hills where old friends waited.

This voyage had been a peaceful one, the ocean behaving itself as if making up for its rough manners two years before. Days passed with never a trace of seasickness. Not even Mella, who claimed to be the world's worst sailor, was ill. For entertainment there had been shuffleboard, matinees for the children, checker tournaments, and outdoor movies at night. Afterward the family had strolled with Sam along deck, listening to the waves splash against the ship and watching the giant lantern of a moon in the sky. If it hadn't been for their eagerness to return home, they could have cruised around the Pacific forever. And something of her father's hunger for the sea had stolen into Paula's spirit.

Now she was tramping down the gangplank, not really studying faces in the crowd below, until a certain blonde head caught her eye.

"Boy!" she said. "That girl sure looks like Virginia

Gillam—only she's too big." Paula had forgotten that time ages everyone.

The next moment the Baileys were in the midst of a loving stampede, the entire Gillam family—their latest addition, Marilyn, included—converging upon them with hugs and kisses. Juanita's soft drawl alone was enough to warm and welcome them in that place of bustling strangers. She and Mella stood back a moment and looked at each other like long-parted sisters.

Beside them stood Ted, big as ever, all smiles, holding the baby on his shoulder. Marilyn was a towhead, her crown a mass of curls, with a beautiful face and the almond eyes of her mother.

All day the two families traveled southward, finally arriving at Point Mugu where Ted was stationed. They visited together for several days, filling in the two-year gap.

Then the Baileys left the Gillams behind and headed for Pomona, a few hours away.

Nearing Pacific Colony, they grew tense with excitement. Palms in clusters waved them on while the hills about them loomed bald against a hot, blue sky.

At last they reached the entrance, Mella looking anxiously around, unmindful of the tailored shrubs and flowers that lined the roadway.

"She's 10 years old now . . ." Mella began. "Couldn't you drive a little faster, Sam?" she pleaded.

"Hey! You don't want me to run over a patient, do you?"

"Of course not! Only—"

"I know, sweetheart. I'm just as eager to see her." He grinned and squeezed his wife's hand.

"Sam, do you think Patty'll remember us?"

Her husband looked thoughtful. "I don't know, Mella. Don't expect her to. After all, two years is quite a spell."

Pulling up near a rambling white building, he parked the car. Shade trees stood everywhere, bowing gracefully over a roof of orange tiles.

"Wait here with your brother, Paula. You can come in

later." Then Mella added, "And don't forget to keep the doors locked."

When the couple entered Patty's room, she lay on her side, facing away from them.

With a lilt to his voice, Sam stood in the doorway and called, "How's Daddy's gal?"

Instantly, Patty flipped over, her saucer eyes wild with joy. "Ah!" she returned, waving her arms excitedly.

She had recognized her father's voice. After two long years clouded with sickness and almost death, she knew him. No one would ever convince Sam otherwise after that moment.

Soon he was cuddling Patty, talking about how pretty she looked. Her eyes spoke back to him, those same dancing eyes that had loved him since she was a baby. He couldn't help but picture her as the toddler she once was, who had greeted him nightly with such vigor, her limbs strong and healthy then.

Mella bent to kiss her, but only distracted her for a moment before Patty gazed up again into her father's face.

"Well, nothing's changed." Mella sighed. "She's still your girl, Sam."

"Yep!"

New spirit entered Mella's voice, "I remember how it used to irk me so. I'd slave all day for her, feeding her, washing and dressing her, and I hardly ever got a response from her. Then you'd come breezing through the door after work, and she'd light up like a Christmas tree. I'd be so jealous!"

Sam chuckled, "I remember." Then he turned to her sympathetically. "Are you jealous now, Mella?"

"Of course not—only happy, happy she remembered. Oh, Sam! She really remembered." Glad tears trickled down Mella's cheeks.

Later Paula was allowed to see Patty, to kiss her, and to stroke her hair that was fast turning brown. She marveled at how tall Patty had grown. Even Little Sam was smuggled in for a few moments. Then they said goodbye and promised to come back soon.

Down the road a few miles Paula asked, "Daddy, why isn't Patty going home with us?"

An uncomfortable silence followed before he explained, "Well, your sister is quite happy there. Did you notice how pretty and contented she looked?"

"Yes."

"And the nurses all love her. Even some of the patients spend a lot of their time talking and singing to her. Think how sad they would be if we took Patty away." Then he added, "Of course, the most important reason is that she's right next to the hospital if she suddenly gets sick again. In fact, her building is kind of like a ward. The doctors check her often. It's really the best place she could stay."

"I guess so, Daddy, but I wish we could see her more."

"I know, princess. Don't worry. We'll visit your sister a lot." Then he turned to Mella. "You know, we should go meet Joyce and her parents now while we're so close."

"Could we?" Mella had been waiting for the chance to meet the woman who had sacrificed her Sundays to play substitute mother to Patty.

They dropped over to Ontario and met Joyce's parents, Mr. and Mrs. Samuelson, a friendly couple. They told the Baileys that Joyce was out walking with her fiancé, Peter. *Fiancé?* Joyce was getting married.

"How wonderful!" Mella exclaimed. "She certainly deserves every happiness."

Joyce finally arrived. She was a tall, slender brunette, and very much like Mella had imagined, although she looked a bit distracted this first meeting. That was understandable, though, with the wedding plans. Joyce did promise to visit Patty on the weekends the family couldn't. Because of the long trip ahead, their meeting was brief. The Baileys said their last goodbye for the day and pointed their Austin in the direction of San Diego.

No structure ever looked so dear to Mella as her home on Chatham Street. There it stood, unchanged, and faithfully awaiting her return.

A regular baby boom had occurred while the Baileys were

away. Their next-door neighbors had a new girl, the Johnsons had evened out their family with two boys, and the Murphys had their Margie, number eight for them.

So there were more children to mind when the punch gatherings resumed at the Bailey house, but it didn't bother the women who were content with one another's company and the brief time-out in their busy day.

Vada, too, fit neatly back into her adopted family as if they had never been away.

One afternoon Mella received a phone call from Dr. Meyers. "Why, Doctor!" she exclaimed. "It's so good to hear your voice. We'll be in to see you next week."

"That's fine, Mrs. Bailey. I'll look forward to your visit." Then he chuckled apologetically. "I hope you don't mind my putting you to work as soon as you're back."

"What do you mean?"

"Well, I have a patient who's literally smothering her retarded child. Nothing I say seems to phase her. I had hoped . . . that is . . . if you could just call her and make her realize how important it is to get help for the boy. He's nine and I'm sure, quite trainable, if only—"

"Say no more, doctor. Just tell me her number."

Mella heard a sigh of relief. "Well, Mrs. Bailey, I see Hawaii hasn't changed you any."

"I hope not," she laughed. "I'm still the same ol' me."

She made the call at once. A conversation followed, much like the one with the deaf boy's mother. When Mella put down the receiver, doubts swamped her. This woman seemed more possessive, so unwilling to give anyone else a chance to train her son.

The following week Mella emerged a happy woman from Dr. Meyers' office. The retarded boy had been enrolled in a special school, and the physician had nothing but praise for Mella and her "friendly persuasion."

That year seemed to race by. Every other Sunday was spent in Pomona with Patty. They were happy journeys, special times for the family. Of course, the children always looked forward to the initial picnic at a Pomona park. It was a lovely place of sprawling, velvety lawns with more playground equipment than the children ever needed.

At Pacific Colony Sam junior and Paula stayed in the car while their parents visited with Patty. The children had plenty of crayons and books to occupy their time, as well as Paula's own runaway imagination that created lively stories about "Black Boulder, the horse." Once in a while, these tales became so involved that she wondered, herself, what the outcome would be.

Checking on her children often, Mella would sit with them awhile and give a report on their sister—how she looked, what she was wearing, her reaction to certain songs. She still loved *Climb, Climb Up Sunshine Mountain* best.

Then, if Paula was fortunate enough, her mother would let her slip in for a brief visit. Those few moments, when the nurses would pretend not to see, were precious. Poor Little Sam! He wasn't as lucky.

One sunny afternoon at Pacific Colony, Paula and her brother lounged in back of their family's newly purchased, used station wagon. The girl was reeling off another horse story, deeply engrossed, when someone knocked on the window.

Expecting her mother, Paula turned eagerly, then gasped. Two large teenage boys were standing there.

"Let us in!" one demanded.

Paula's young heart thumped with fear as she scanned the locks. They were down, so she breathed easier.

"No!" the girl replied, trying to assume a certain calmness for her brother's benefit.

Paula watched them stalk around the front of the car to the passenger side. When that door failed to open, a hand slipped through the small gap atop the window. Further and further it went. She wondered if he would reach the lock.

"Go away!" the girl shouted. "My mother's coming any minute. You'll be sorry."

The arm stopped, and she realized it was stuck and couldn't squeeze through another inch. After retrieving the arm with some difficulty, the boy and his companion started around the car.

*The rear door! It's not fastened.* Paula scooted back and clicked it just in time.

Then she heard the most beautiful sound—her mother's voice. Although it was nervously loud, it was still music to the girl. "What do you boys think you're doing?"

"We want some nickels to get candy in the machine," one said.

"Well, you won't find any nickels in there," Mella told them pleasantly. By that time she realized the teenagers were patients and weren't really responsible.

The boys hung around awhile, hoping the woman would give them the money. At last they went limping away, muttering to themselves.

"Oh, Mama! I was so afraid."

Mella's arms trembled around Paula. "I know, darling. But you were very good not to open the door. I'm so proud of you."

"Well, I wasn't scared," boasted Sam junior. He couldn't understand what all the fuss was about.

Mella took out a handkerchief and dried her daughter's face. "How would you like to go in now and see your sister, young lady?"

"Oh, yes!" Paula said excitedly. That was all the comforting she needed.

When she stole into Patty's room, she noticed her sister looking especially pretty that day, more radiant than ever, with her hand tightly clasped around her father's. After a few words and kisses, Paula left, turning for a moment in the doorway to get one last glimpse of Patty's face.

That evening, after the children were tucked in their beds, Mella fled to her empty bedroom and wept. She had been saving those tears all afternoon, ever since the incident in the parking lot. She would never again feel safe about leaving Little Sam and Paula alone in the car.

What could she do? There were neighbors, of course. But Mella, ever independent, hated to think of imposing on them and tying up their weekends. *No*, she decided. *They've done too much for me already*.

Mella never had to solve her problem. Her daughter's lifelong enemy, pneumonia, finally triumphed. Patty's time with them was over.

The news of the girl's death spread quickly through Fletcher Hills, bringing a flood of sympathizers and food to the house on Chatham Street.

Mom Bert flew from the East Coast to weep gently at her granddaughter's coffin, while the Italian relatives mourned openly in loud, unrestrained sobbing. Mella clung to her uniformed husband who, as always, remained her strength.

One person, however, seemed unmoved by the emotional display around her—10-year-old Paula. Her placid smile could be attributed to something that had happened a few nights earlier.

When the fateful news had reached the Bailey family, Paula had accompanied her tearful mother to Coronado Island to retrieve her father from what should have been night duty.

Before, when Paula had stood on the deck of the ferry and gazed into the wake, fantasies would emerge, happy daydreams that could occupy any child during a ferry boat ride. But that night the waters were unfriendly. Death had claimed Paula's sister, and across the bay Coronado's scattered lights dotted a mourning veil of sky and sea.

*Daddy's over there somewhere*, she thought, *talking with some sailors, but keeping the hurt to himself*.

She recalled her last visit with Patty, the round face, the dark eyes, the song in her voice. Paula knew Patty's story well, all the lives the invalid had touched. In some instances her sister was better than the most stirring sermon, because she mellowed people, teaching them in her own silent way. Paula knew, with a wisdom beyond her years, that Patty had shaped the person she was and the adult she would eventually become.

The floor rocked unsteadily beneath her as the ferry

docked. When Paula scurried back to the car she noticed her mother's eyes were dry, but still showing her sadness. Paula wanted to share her reverie, tell her mother how Patty's life wasn't a waste, point out all the people—from minister to alcoholic—who were enriched by Patty's presence.

When Paula tried to talk, though, she found herself strangely tongue-tied, but the awful loss drew them close to each other. She realized there was no need for words just then. In time, she would tell her mother.

The car lurched forward, making its careful way onto Coronado Island where her father waited. Outside, the trees cast giant shadows across a moonlit road, but inside Paula enjoyed a light of her own, one that revealed purpose in her sister's short life. To Paula, that was all that mattered.

# EPILOGUE

After Sam Bailey retired from the Navy in 1957, he and his wife moved to Maryland with Paula, Sam junior, and their latest son, Roger. Another daughter, Carmelita (Carme) would be born in the East, completing the family.

Although the Baileys live now in Cary, North Carolina, their home still buzzes with constant activity as more grand-children are added to the flock and neighbors drop by regularly.

Paula, the author of this book, keeps in touch with her parents from Washington state where she lives with her logger-husband and two college-aged children.

Sam junior, a graduate of Western Carolina University, works for an airline company in San Antonio, Texas.

Mella Bailey continues to cross denominational lines as she helps her husband in his Protestant church, their uncomplicated faith still touching the many who are welcomed into their home.

# Refreshing Accounts of God's Healing Grace

**Forsake Me Not**
Devastated by a broken engagement and feeling betrayed by God, Megan leaves everything behind to try teaching at a New York City church school. There she meets Mike—a youth pastor determined to convince her that God *is* leading and that accepting a date with him just might be part of His plan. Before long the couple fall in love. Then suddenly a violent wreck shatters their plans, and Mike wants to end the relationship. But Megan won't give up. Having learned that the Lord will never leave her, she pleads with God for help. His answer, while not what she expects, is beyond her wildest dreams! By Kay Rizzo. Paper, 156 pages. US$7.95 Cdn$9.95.

**The Heart Remembers**
A daughter, mother, and grandmother find themselves separated by a painful and abusive past. Yearning for acceptance, yet withholding forgiveness from each other as punishment, they realize their cherished grudges have locked them away from each other. This poignant story about forgiveness reveals how God's unconditional love can free us to let go of our painful past. By Helen Godfrey Pyke. Paper, 108 pages. US$7.95, Cdn$9.95.

**Love's Bitter Victory**
How do you tell your child you're sorry for missing the first 24 years of his life? Laura Michaels begins a journey away from alcoholism and discovers Jesus, a new start with her son, and a joy so contagious that it begins to change the broken lives around her. By Midge Nayler. Paper, 187 pages. US$8.95, Cdn$11.20.

---

To order, call **1-800-765-6955** or write to ABC Mailing Service, P.O. Box 1119, Hagerstown, MD 21741. Send check or money order. Enclose applicable sales tax and 15 percent (minimum US$2.50) for postage and handling. Prices and availability subject to change without notice. Add 7 percent GST in Canada.

# Compelling Conversion Stories

**April Showers**
When Eric walks out on April, leaving her with three tiny
children, tremendous bills, and no way to make a decent income,
she doesn't have the slightest idea how to manage on her own.
But as the months pass, her grief turns to anger, then action.
Along the way she discovers a friend in her heavenly Father and
an unexpected romance. By VeraLee Wiggins. Paper, 125 pages.
US$6.95, Cdn$8.70.

**The Heart and Soul of Landon Harris**
It had all been a mistake, Landon thought. Leaving Joetta,
marrying power-hungry Diana, then divorcing her. Spending 15
years in that cutthroat engineering job. He was sick of the rat
race and guilt. All that mattered now were his son and stepson,
and that he might lose them. He desperately wanted to start
over, and God was his only hope. This is a compelling story
about a single father's quest for God and new beginnings with
his family. By Helen Godfrey Pyke. Paper, 140 pages. US$7.95,
Cdn$9.95.

**My Father's Bitter Gift**
Archie vowed he would never be like his father, yet the time
came when he realized alcohol was leading him down the same
path. A story of hope, this book reveals God's saving grace to
free people from developed and inherited tendencies. By Dorothy
Eaton Watts. Paper, 95 pages. US$6.95, Cdn$8.70.

---

To order, call **1-800-765-6955** or write to ABC Mailing Service, P.O. Box
1119, Hagerstown, MD 21741. Send check or money order. Enclose
applicable sales tax and 15 percent (minimum US$2.50) for postage and
handling. Prices and availability subject to change without notice. Add 7
percent GST in Canada.